RESURRECTING
THE DEAD

WE NOW KNOW MORE ABOUT BILLY THE KID THE PERSON THAN THE LEGEND

RESURRECTING
THE DEAD

Dale L. Tunnell, Ph.D.

Western Legends Research, LLC

Western Legends Research, LLC
P. O. Box
Sun City West, AZ 85376
www.WesternLegendsResearch.com

Copyright © 2019 Dale L. Tunnell, Ph.D.

Any references to historical events, real people, or real places are used fictitiously. Names, characters, and places are products of the author's imagination.

All rights reserved. No part of this publication may be reproduced, distributed, or transmitted in any form or by any means, including photocopying, recording, or other electronic or mechanical methods, without the prior written permission of the publisher, except in the case of brief quotations embodied in critical reviews and certain other noncommercial uses permitted by copyright law. For permission requests, write to the publisher, addressed "Attention: Permissions Coordinator," at the address above.

Front cover image and book design by The Book Cover Whisperer: ProfessionalBookCoverDesign.com

Printed by Western Legends Research, LLC,
in the United States of America

Library of Congress Control Number: 2019912284

ISBN: 978-1-7334212-0-1 Paperback
ISBN: 978-1-7334212-1-8 eBook
ISBN: 978-1-7334212-2-5 Kindle

FIRST EDITION

*I Dedicate this Book to My
Loving and Devoted Wife and Partner,
Deborah Lynn Tunnell*

TABLE OF CONTENTS

FOREWORD i
PREFACE v
INTRODUCTION vii
PART I: PROFILING BILLY THE KID 1
CHAPTER 1: A Brief History 3
    The Death of Catherine Antrim 4
    Onward to Wichita 6
    Life in Silver City 8
    Death of "Windy" Cahill 8
    The "Chain Gang" 10
    Prelude to the Lincoln County War 12
    Death of John Tunstall 18
    The Regulators 21
    Blazer's Mill 24
    The Indictments 25
    Battle of Fritz Ranch 26
    Taking on a New Enemy 27
    Battle of Lincoln 29
    On to Fort Sumner 30
    A New Governor 31
    The Kid's Survival 33
    Death of "Texas Red" 34
    Stinking Springs 35
    The Trial 39
    The Escape 39

The Final Shot	42
CHAPTER 2: An Unproven Death	50
CHAPTER 3: Abandonment and Loyalties Lost	60
CHAPTER 4: An Adolescent Life	68
CHAPTER 5: Anatomy as Evidence	76
CHAPTER 6: Content Analysis of Verbal Behavior	85
W. H. Bonney Letter to Friend Wilson, March 20, 1879	87
Letter fragment by Billie, 1879	87
W.H. Bonney Letter to Lew Wallace, March 20, 1879	89
William Bonney Letter to Lew Wallace, December 12, 1880	91
W. H. Bonney Note to Lew Wallace, January 1, 1881	94
Wm. H. Bonney Letter to Lew Wallace, March 4, 1881	94
W. Bonney Note to Lew Wallace, March 27, 1881	96
The Analysis	96
PART II: UNMASKING THE IMPOSTER	109
CHAPTER 7: Exhumation of John Miller	111
CHAPTER 8: The Pretender	122
A Faulty Foundation	124
The Drive to Ramah	127
A Matrimonial Union	130
Herman Tecklenburg	131
Eugene Lambson	131
Isadora's Death and the Mysterious Trunk	133
The Probate Mystery	134
Too Many Wounds	136
A Rapid Departure	138
The Ontario Provincial Police Inspector	139
Who Was Isadora Miller?	147
CHAPTER 9: Imposter Unmasked	152

CHAPTER 10: Ambush at Stoneville, Montana 160
CHAPTER 11: The Next Man in Line 174
EPILOGUE 177
APPENDICES 179
ACKNOWLEDGEMENTS 201
BIBLIOGRAPHY 203
INDEX 217
ABOUT THE AUTHOR 231

TABLE OF FIGURES

Figure 1. Jesse Evans with an Unknown Woman 11

Figure 2. Lawrence Murphy 13

Figure 3. James Dolan 13

Figure 4. John Henry Tunstall 20

Figure 5. Dick Brewer 22

Figure 6. Sheriff William Brady 23

Figure 7. Charlie Bowdre 26

Figure 8. Thomas B. Catron 28

Figure 9. Governor Lew Wallace 32

Figure 10. Patrick Floyd Garrett 36

Figure 11. Tom O'Folliard 38

Figure 12. Samuel B. Axtell 40

Figure 13. Robert Olinger 42

Figure 14. William H. Bonney Alias Billy the Kid 78

Figure 15. Ear Morphology Diagram 81

Figure 16. The Arizona Republic 120

Figure 17. William H. Bonney Alias Billy the Kid 153

Figure 18. John Miller about 50 Years of Age 155

Figure 19. John Miller Wearing a Pistol 166

Figure 20. John Miller Wearing Leather Chaps 167

Figure 21. George Exelbee 169

FOREWORD

WHAT WOULD IT BE LIKE in a world where the ordinary man or woman could quickly unmask impostors and miscreants of society; where they could openly expose with proven scientific accuracy, the guile, and cunning of criminal behavior? Well, let me introduce you to Dr. Dale Tunnell.

It was 2004 when the hot and seasonal California fires were burning at their full potential, and a veil of smoke hung in the air. I was staying at the Best Western just off Kettleman Lane in Lodi, California when I heard a knock at my door. When I opened the door, in walked a rather large man who had the look of a seasoned law enforcement professional, clearly a confident man. He shook my hand in a firm grip and said, "Howdy Brian. I'm Dale Tunnell."

I was going through an extremely contentious legal battle at the time, and I contacted Dale and asked him for help in unmasking my adversary's hidden personality. I sent Dale every single email and voice message my opponent sent me. Dale spent several weeks analyzing the language and character of each communication. The result was a comprehensive narrative that identified a narcissistic and abusive personality to the point of a near clinical diagnosis. Dale handed me the multi-page report and in a soft voice said, "Brian, I hope this helps you."

I was shocked! He was accurate in every aspect of the behavior. What he described in his report identified all those behaviors that had not been apparent to me. He explained in detail my adversary's intellect, irrationality, motives, and most importantly, he predicted the danger I faced. It was all there. To put it mildly, I was astounded that my adversary concealed in their language so much information. It became evident that Dale had examined every word said. He linked linguistic patterns with feigned displays of anger and outrage to produce a highly accurate psychological portrait of a person who was a serial abuser and pathological liar.

I learned everyone is literally, an open book if one knows what to analyze. And Dale does! He is an expert in a highly advanced methodology often used in national security and criminal inquiries. What this technology exposes about a person is both reasoned and revealing. Using language patterns, Dale not only profiles the person but by examining their verbal behavior, he peers deeply into their innermost secrets. Language is verbal behavior and it provides the means to recognize conviction, concealed details, malintent, and personality traits.

Dale is an expert and combined with his training, education and many years as a criminal investigator and intelligence professional, nothing gets past him. Evaluating their recorded language, Dale brings long-dead legendary personalities back to life.

Now, many of our historical figures are about to get a rude awaking from beyond the grave and will no longer be able to rest on their often conveniently recorded representation in history.

With Dale's skill and experience, we are about to learn not just the truth, but the evidence behind it as well. Can you imagine the potential to affect our views on history and our world today! We can now learn how these people felt and what troubled them; understand their ailments and pathology. What caused them to suffer, and how did they react? By following Dale, we discover who they were, regardless of reputation.

This book, *Resurrecting the Dead*, has something to satisfy everyone. If you like history, you will acquire individual facts about Billy the Kid you might not have known. If you are into psychology, his analysis will produce an image of the real William H. Bonney not otherwise disclosed. If technology is your thing, understanding how Dale utilized his skills will impress you. If you are a western legends fan, you will develop a full new comprehension of the landscape and environment in which these characters thrived.

This book is a historical crime mystery. It is as if the characters got up out of the pages and sat across from you and told you their life's secrets; their victories and disappointments still rich and raw with experiences and feelings of their time.

Dale has created a masterpiece. As he did for me many years ago when he helped me unmask my enemy, he demonstrated that the words are alive with clues and connections.

Dr. Dale Tunnell has advanced beyond the level of profiler or investigator. He has become a modern "*language inquisitor*" with a magnifying glass and a computer. I wonder what legend the "*Inquisitor*" will unmask next? Will he find out what was inside John Miller's mystery trunk? Will Dale find evidence to solve the unproven death? What did Isadora Miller know and from where did she come? Was it John Miller's fate to assume the role of one of America's most prominent western legends only to die alone without fame? What mysterious part did George Exelbee and a gun battle in a tiny settlement in Eastern Montana play in this saga?

Dale found many of the answers, and they are all within the language of the legends!

BRIAN IAN RICHARD CALDER
LONDON, ENGLAND
8:42 PM 8/1/2019

PREFACE

"I DON'T CARE WHAT anybody says. Billy the Kid was killed in Fort Sumner, New Mexico, on July 14th, 1881, by Pat Garrett, and they buried the Kid in the Fort Sumner Cemetery," a refrain often expressed by historians and laypersons alike.

It is human nature to believe seemingly compelling stories in addition to rationalizing with conviction that which complements personal agendas. To some degree, we are all susceptible. It takes sincere effort to investigate and methodically evaluate any information that has been provided to support an established bias.

Opposing views are products of curious minds, and without reasoned opposition, society becomes an autonomic sponge. Of course, humans are fallible. Because something sounds reasonable, our own biases and uninformed opinions create channels of acceptance. When we miss something essential, it's because we are not looking deeply enough. Not much has changed since the days of Billy the Kid in that respect.

So I asked the question, "What is wrong with questioning the accuracy of history?" Especially history that is more than one hundred years old. It may be as simple as this: change is a difficult concept for some people. In some instances, the barricaded-belief model has not transformed in the past 150 years and often drives the narrative in media, politics, and public opinion of today.

An investigation isn't rocket science. It is an endeavor that requires effort, sometimes extreme effort, expending exhaustive hours in thought and analysis, and curiosity from deep within one's soul. My journey with William H. Bonney, alias Billy the Kid, and his impostors has been an enlightening one and indeed very interesting. I hope my findings stimulate others to explore facts buried in the minutia of the Old West and of those who made history. Maybe the accounts in this book will contribute to your ongoing curiosity and launch your participation in the enduring debates of American Western legends and the remarkable stories of resilience and capitulation.

INTRODUCTION

AFTER LEAVING THE U.S. Army in 1976, my first job in law enforcement was with the Lincoln County Sheriff's Department in Lincoln County, New Mexico. Low pay and lots of miles to cover, I didn't stay long. There were only a sheriff, undersheriff and four deputies to cover over forty-six-hundred square miles of desert, mountains, forest, and ranch land. I was the only deputy in the northern half of the county separated from the rest of the county by the Capitan Mountains. My only backup was a New Mexico State patrolman who had retired in place, and a handful of volunteers of the New Mexico Mounted Patrol.

I learned at this point that the Old West was still alive and well in Lincoln County, and not much had changed in the way of lawlessness. Outlaws still existed, only with a little more criminal sophistication and a higher standard of living. There was rustling—with cattle trucks instead of driving herds to hideouts. Murders weren't as frequent, but because of so many remote locations, it was still easy to hide the bodies. Fraud and corruption by politicians and land barons remained a primary method to steal from folks. Because we had so few deputies, it was difficult to investigate, prosecute, and gain convictions. Money and power were ever-present, and some enjoyed protected status, not unlike the days of the corrupt Santa Fe Ring.

Organized crime moved in and drugs, theft, and burglary-for-hire were mainstay methods for acquiring ill-gotten wealth. I understand from friends who still live there that generations later, many resident families continue to follow the outlaw path. It was and is a beautiful country, and while I was not very interested at the time in Lincoln County history, I did visit many of the same haunts of desperados from the late 1800s. From the Sacramento mountains to the northern county line and from the Pecos River to the Malpais, I traveled throughout the country visiting with ranchers whose families were original pioneers. They told me stories and showed me relics handed down from their grandparents. You could not move about without crossing some historic piece of ground. A fantastic time, I miss it now.

Forty-three years later, I realize that despite low pay and long hours, that job may have been the best I ever had in law enforcement. It took me nearly thirty years to gain interest in the Lincoln County War and especially Billy the Kid. I certainly did not know at the time of my first law enforcement job that I would become so fascinated by events and intrigue of the Lincoln County War.

After reading hundreds of articles, web pages, and books about Billy the Kid, I have concluded that nearly all accounts begin with a rehash of Billy's history from puberty to his death. The same information with only minor deviations continues in presentation, almost as a filler to make pages in manuscripts and texts. So much has been written about the Kid's life that one can easily recognize narratives and familiar stories without referencing a single book.

Is this rehash of old information useful? I believe it is! Anecdotes and verified details about Billy the Kid provide a reader with a frame of reference. Without some historical framework, it may be challenging to grasp the full personality of one of the most written-about outlaws in the history of the American West. While my description of Billy's life may be more suggestive of snapshots, there is a substantial accumulation of research performed by authors such as Robert

Utley, Leon Metz, Frederick Nolan, and many others who labored for over a century to paint an accurate picture of the Kid from birth to death. There are some missteps, and occasionally, the details conflict. But overall, a reasonable person can at least surmise that Billy lived a tragic life, maybe of his own accord.

Most historians like to commence their evaluations at Billy's origin and proceed with narratives along intersecting paths of documented history, relying on personal accounts, newspaper clippings and researchers who have toiled before them. Not as a historian but as an investigator of many years and experiences, I prefer to examine known points of reference and backtrack historical data until I reach dead ends. I find that gaps in historical knowledge are more apparent and not hidden among hyperbole and conjecture. By using this method, we can more easily separate what we can prove from what we suspect. Rather than recreate another in-depth historical text, I consulted existing works and provided illustrations of those captured critical segments of Billy the Kid's life. Numerous books were rich in details and provided an overview, so to speak, for an examination of nearly twenty years of Billy's development.

This book isn't just about the life and times of Billy the Kid, though. I am writing about a factual and historical crime mystery in which an impersonator assumes the identity of an outlaw legend. Chronicled background provides the turf on which to use scientific methodology; to perform a psychological autopsy on one personality and discover supporting evidence to dispute the claim of another.

For 137 years authors have written hundreds of articles and books about William H. Bonney, alias Billy the Kid. Debate and argument still rage about whether he was killed that night on July 14th, 1881, or did a vast conspiracy strive to hide his survival. Regardless of whether one is a historian, a researcher, or merely a storyteller, it is nearly overwhelming to consider how much information, true or not, exists about the Kid. The real task is to sort through all that information and identify what is legitimate and discard what is not.

Considering the scarcity of accurate documentation, determining what is right and what is not becomes a real dilemma. Stories are told by many who said they were participants in a historical event, or they had first-hand knowledge of personalities. There has not been a means to evaluate and confirm the validity of those accounts until now. Then, of course, there are also the countless stories passed down through genealogical trees told by relatives and pioneers, some with a bit of embellishment to exaggerate their family members' importance or simply the relating of a family folktale. The task to elucidate fact from fiction seems daunting, but it's not entirely impossible.

I prefer deductive reasoning, critical thinking, and modern methodology, to examine these stories and to determine if they are reasonable based on each of their own merits. Relying on accurate documentation and scientific methodology helps to flush out facts. Do these methods bring everything to light? Not always, but it is a good beginning and points to a reasoned planning process. A researcher is often left with only a gut feeling as to what transpired, and frequently, the legend is more interesting than the truth. Researchers are known to get it wrong. But they also get it right. And, sometimes, we find details that uncover facts hidden in history. But remember, authors, are never the decision-makers. That is the sole responsibility of readers.

In this book, I will discuss previous findings and efforts by others to prove or disprove them. Often global statements were made about evidentiary findings that while they are of importance in the debate, they cannot be generalized and accepted as absolute conclusions. It's also essential for the reader to have a frame of reference to help understand the nature of those about whom we write. I have provided an overview with enough detail to meet that need.

I also present details of critical importance about Billy the Kid's anatomy which may be used to exclude those who claim to be him after his alleged miraculous escape from death at the hands of Sheriff Pat Garrett. These details are scientific, and they represent recent medical and pathological assessments accepted by both pathologists and physicians alike. Also, medical research within the last ten years represents a substantially new understanding of adolescent brain development and the effects of congenital disorders. There are physiological, pathological, and psychological contributors to the Kid's overall growth and the making of his personality.

I examine psychological and cognitive dispositions that were the basis of his evolution from youth to adulthood. Billy's few writings to Governor Lew Wallace and others, provide vital channels of evaluation in the way he used his words and how he expressed himself. The latest assessment technology helps to identify his mental states, cognitive abilities, and any psychiatric conditions that affected his decision-making. The details gleaned from my efforts represent both real and material revelations. They represent results of validated research-testing methods and accepted investigative methodology recognized by thousands of law enforcement agencies worldwide. As a legislator once said on the topic of impeaching Richard Nixon, "My mind is made up. Don't confuse me with the facts." It is the reader's right to challenge the evidence and draw conclusions from the weight of details they deem essential.

In summary, based on my education, experience, and

training, I can stipulate only that which I have determined to be necessary. I fervently hope that readers will search for more answers to either support positions I advance or refute them. I have no agenda other than to present facts and set records straight where I can. I hope you enjoy this book and find some things you didn't already know. In some instances, I can almost guarantee your astonishment, and hopefully, my insights will provide the impetus for a new understanding of the making of Billy the Kid.

PART I:

PROFILING BILLY THE KID

CHAPTER 1

A Brief History

FREDERICK NOLAN SUMMED up our knowledge of Billy the Kid's beginnings in his book, *The West of Billy the Kid*. He intimated that researchers have been at it for over a century, and the knowledge they have developed about Billy's origin can be categorized like this: possibly, probably, maybe, potentially, oh never mind! Here's a fact. There is no record of birth, no record of who his father was, no genealogy, no demographic data. Some patterns match some of what we suspect about him, but they generally fall apart under intense scrutiny. Researchers have relied on news clippings and census records to build profiles that are merely conjecture-based, and if you read that someone has absolutely proven the Kid's date of birth and where he was born, they may as well be placing a For Sale sign on the Brooklyn bridge to get your attention. You are more likely to take possession of the bridge before anyone accurately identifies the Kid's heredity.[1]

Records were minimal at best during the era of Billy the Kid, and frequently, they were absent. Researchers often learn of critical data by stumbling onto it from dusty tomes hidden in courthouse basements and historical collections containing thousands of documents. Having myself performed numerous hand-searches of letters, family records, newspaper archives, census records, and government reports, I am always amazed at the gems of information I have discovered. Quite often, though, other researchers have been there before me.

Concerning documentation, we haven't been so lucky in determining Billy's birth data. Some believe he was born on November 23, 1859, in New York City.[2] Others place his origin in Indiana or Coffeyville, Kansas.[3] His mother was Catherine McCarty, but no one knows for sure from where she came. Was her maiden name "Bonney" or was it something else? Was Billy's father's name William Henry McCarty? Did he die after Billy was born? Was there a divorce that caused family separation? Realistically, there have been no absolutes. Searching through census records produced hundreds of entries containing the names of McCarty and Bonney, and though some combinations seemed to have contributed to grand journalistic theory, the corroboration is missing.

Not knowing Billy's date of birth creates somewhat of a dilemma. When we find some record of his activities, his age is often undetermined. For instance, we do not know how old Billy was when he departed Silver City after his mother died. We have a date range from accounts provided by people who knew him. They proffered that he was around twelve years old. If you believe he was born in New York in 1859, he was closer to fifteen. So, let's use his mother's date of death as a point of reference and move around the old board a bit.

The Death of Catherine Antrim

Young Henry Antrim or Henry McCarty lost his mother to tuberculosis at a time when he probably needed her most. His stepfather was mostly absent, and by all accounts, he provided little or no parental support to young Henry. Because he was so young when his mother died, the impact of losing her certainly contributed significantly to his social decline. That moment in his life is perhaps the best time to begin the unmasking of Billy the Kid.

Catherine McCarty Antrim died on September 16, 1874, and the annals of Silver City, New Mexico history documented her passing well.[4] Her departure left her sons, Henry and Josie, without sustenance and shelter, though the boys' stepfather, Henry Antrim, eventually arranged for them to work in exchange for their room and board, then abandoned them. A critical period for Henry, without real adult supervision he joined the "Street Arabs," a group of unsupervised mischievous kids known to pull pranks and commit petty theft. It was only a few years from this date Henry would become known as Billy the Kid. Many residents who knew Henry described him as a young boy, small in stature, 75 pounds, and about ten to twelve years old when he arrived in Silver City. His mother enrolled him in school, and by all accounts, Henry took a liking to the schoolteacher. He seemed to be an engaging student and no wilder than any other student during this time.[5]

There is clear evidence that Catherine McCarty married William H. Antrim at the Presbyterian church in Santa Fe, New Mexico on March 1, 1873. Listed among witnesses to the marriage were Henry and Joseph McCarty.[6] As a family now, they departed Santa Fe and arrived in Silver City in the early summer. While the Antrim family was able to secure suitable lodging, many new immigrants and miners lived in tents, and thousand more newcomers arrived within the next several months. Intending on building a new life, Catherine Antrim began a laundry service, and William Henry Antrim decided to engage in mining and prospecting. Both boys enrolled in school, but neither probably suspected they would find themselves alone and without support within a year. Anecdotal information about the boys' time in Silver City seemed, for the most part, to agree. The boys moved from a structured environment to an unstructured one and became involved in limited gang-like activity with more attention paid to young Henry than to Joseph.

Onward to Wichita

Before Henry Antrim and Catherine McCarty took their marital vows in Santa Fe, New Mexico in 1873, no one knows from where they came. Later in Joseph Antrim's life, he reflected that the Antrim and McCarty Group traveled from Kansas to Denver and then on to Santa Fe, but there is no evidence to support his recollections. There is a gap in their travel history between a confirmed date of Catherine's sale of her property in Wichita, Kansas on August 25, 1871, until they arrived in Santa Fe in 1873, and only conjecture places the group in Denver, Colorado

What is more important to me is that there is a two-year gap of information confirming the location, timeframe, and life efforts of the McCarty family and Antrim. Once again, there is a deficit in the amount of legitimate information available to establish the family endeavors during this period. In other words, this is one of those gaps I referred to earlier. Whether it's critical or not remains to be discovered. It would interest me to find out whether Catherine's tuberculosis was in full swing and what influences her sickness had on their travels. Did they go to Denver for her treatment, or was it a stopover for their journey to New Mexico and a dryer climate?

While we know little of their journey and this two-year gap in time, there is ample supporting evidence they were traveling from Wichita, Kansas. There are numerous documents and attestations that Catherine and William took advantage of the Osage Indian Trust Act of 1869. While nothing can be presented to explain why twenty-three-year-old William Antrim was attracted to thirty-five-year-old Catherine McCarty, they developed a mutually satisfying relationship in Indianapolis, Indiana and moved from there to Wichita in 1870.[7]

There was not a lot of documentation to build an accurate picture of their lives in Wichita, but there was enough to show they owned property there and that Catherine was somewhat engaged in local politics. In an event dated July 21, 1870, a petition for the incorporation of Wichita included Catherine's name which suggested she had designs of becoming more than a housewife.[8] Within a year or so Antrim and the McCarty family acquired property, and Catherine engaged in an established business. More importantly to me was what little Henry and Joseph were doing while William and Catherine worked. Were they in school or just helping mom out at the laundry? Again, information is lacking. However, if the description of Henry's age upon arrival in Silver City was accurate by those who went to school with him, then he was only about eight to nine years old while living in Wichita.

There is much speculation that Henry and Joseph were half-brothers and that Joseph was born nearly two years after Henry. Except for Catherine McCarty appearing in local directories around 1867 in Indianapolis, not one other single shred of evidence exists to prove who the father or fathers were of either Henry or Joseph. Once again, the reference to Henry's age in Silver City puts him at about six in Indianapolis. Continuing this reverse aging pattern, he would have been born closer to 1861 rather than 1859 like so many believed.

A reader might ask why Henry's paternal history is so important and why is his birth in 1861 rather than 1859 is so significant. The answers will be more apparent later but for now, the difference of two years and the name Bonney are highly substantial elements in the making of Billy the Kid, alias William H. Bonney.

Life in Silver City

Moving forward in time from Catherine's death in September of 1874, it was clear that Henry's life was about to take a turn for the worse. He became a member of a group of street urchins known as the "Village Arabs," and he was becoming increasingly more delinquent. With no parental guidance, he was free to follow his path, regardless of where it led. By all accounts, he remained in Silver City into 1875. The county sheriff, Whitehill, arrested Henry during this time for stealing laundry from a local Chinese proprietor and placed him in the jail. Worried he would be there until the next district court date in December, Henry climbed the chimney and escaped.

While there are several accounts without confirmation as to what he did next, Henry eventually ended up in Arizona, possibly meeting with his stepfather. How that meeting turned out is uncertain, but in due course, he ended up at Camp Goodwin, Arizona near San Carlos reservation where he stole a cavalry horse. From there, Henry rode to Fort Grant looking for work. There was some thought that during this time he may have returned to Wichita, Kansas for some reason but being as young as he was when he and his family lived there, the motivation for that trip seems questionable. For nearly a year, another gap in information, Henry avoided a public record. By the fall of 1876, Henry returned to the Fort Grant country, specifically in the area of Bonita, Arizona. It was during this timeframe that Henry picked up the moniker, "Kid."[9]

Death of "Windy" Cahill

While in the Bonita, Arizona area, an ex-cavalryman, John R. Mackie befriended the Kid and showed him how to steal horses, horse blankets and saddles from soldiers visiting local prostitutes. Over a year or so, several escapades occurred while Henry, now known as "Kid Antrim," was in and around Fort

Grant.[10] The descriptions may or may not have been accurate, but what is known is that on August 17, 1877, the Kid tangled with a blacksmith named Frank "Windy" Cahill. The Kid was playing poker at George Atkins's cantina when he became involved in an altercation with Cahill. Cahill was known to be a bully, and he frequently abused the Kid. Eventually, Cahill held Henry in a bear hug as they wrestled outside by the chutes behind the cantina. Pinning Henry on the ground, Cahill was calling the Kid names and slapping him. Henry was able to reach for a gun he had positioned in his trousers and shoot Cahill in the stomach. Henry made his escape by stealing a horse known for his speed while Cahill was taken to the post infirmary for treatment by the post surgeon.

Cahill provided a dying declaration to document the episode. Lying in agony of a stomach gunshot wound, Cahill eventually succumbed to the injury. A coroner's jury ultimately ruled that the shooting had been "criminal and unjustifiable and that Henry Antrim alias Kid is guilty thereof."[11] While this event may have been a clear case of self-defense due to their differences in size and age, Henry probably would not have received fair consideration as a result of Cahill's affiliations. Subsequently, the Kid, now known as "Billy the Kid" alias Kid Antrim, and on the run, lit out for New Mexico with no money, no home, and no friends. Along the way, the Kid became affiliated with a group of killers and rustlers known as the "Chain Gain," so known for their ability as an organized ring of thieves, to move stolen animals from one link in the chain to the next. Tracking stolen cattle and horses became impossible due to the numerous handoffs from one group to another. His burgeoning relationship in September 1877 with "the Boys" led by Jesse Evans who was active in the "Chain Gang," no doubt provided him with a superb education in stealing livestock.[12]

The "Chain Gang"

Throughout the remainder of 1877, the Kid, now calling himself Billy Bonney, engaged in numerous occurrences of cattle rustling and theft, but he also made a few new friends. Whenever the coffers went dry and further funding was needed, the Boys stole whatever livestock they required. Their thievery was so prolific and hazardous for them; it became necessary to move on to greener and much safer pastures. So, they moved their operations into Lincoln County. The abundance of cattle ranches made the country a target-rich environment. Their methods were the same; work in bands of two or four from different outlaw groups and move the livestock to prearranged locations. Banding herds together, the rustled cattle and horses were moved to other places for sale.[13]

On September 18, 1877, the Boys stole several horses belonging to John Tunstall, Alexander McSween and Dick Brewer. Among those taken were a dapple-grey buggy team belonging to Tunstall. With several pursuers close behind, the Boys moved the horses to a ranch belonging to Jimmy McDaniels. Individuals who would eventually become close friends of the Kid, Dick Brewer, Doc Scurlock, and Charlie Bowdre, were in hot pursuit of the stolen animals and determined to get them back. At one point, Dick Brewer rode into the Boys' camp and tried to negotiate the return of the horses, but Jesse Evans laughed off the attempt only offering Brewer's horses back to him. Brewer declined the offer telling Evans that if he couldn't recover Tunstall's horses also, Evans could keep them and go to hell.[14]

The Boys continued west, stealing and disposing of more animals through the "Chain Gang" and then reversed directions continuing their livestock theft, heading back to Lincoln County. By this time, Billy Bonney alias Billy the Kid was known and recognized as a member of the Evan's gang.

Figure 1. Jesse Evans with an unknown woman. (Unknown photography studio.) Public domain.

The "chain gang" had become so versatile during 1877 that they moved with impunity throughout southern New Mexico and Arizona. Back and forth, they traveled, stealing and selling livestock whenever the opportunity presented. In October of that year, while moving back through La Mesilla, New Mexico, Billy took a pony belonging to the daughter of Sheriff Mariano Barela. Considering his age at the time, between fourteen and sixteen years of age, he probably wasn't making the best decisions of his life. The theft of a horse belonging to a sheriff's daughter was most likely one of those poor decisions. It was bad enough to steal from a sheriff but to bring tears to his daughter over the loss of her pony was more than the sheriff could abide. Vengeance is mine sayeth a father of a crying daughter![15]

Prelude to the Lincoln County War

While the purloining of livestock continued unchecked throughout the Southwest, a battle was raging in Lincoln County among ranchers and thieves. John Chisum, Cattle King of the Southwest, was losing cattle by the hundreds and he was intent on stopping the thievery. Chisum was declaring war on the thieves. No trial. Just kill them. His declaration of hostilities was an effort to maintain his monopoly of grassland and water, but it encouraged other unsavory ranchers who were fighting for their survival to align themselves with L. G. Murphy & Company and Jimmy Dolan of Lincoln. The Murphy-Dolan camp backed by the Santa Fe Ring and Governor Axtell was intent on supplying beef to Indian reservation and army contracts from their "miracle herd," known for never decreasing no matter how many cattle they sold.[16] Chisum knew that his herd was being decimated by either Jesse Evans and the Boys or by other ranchers supported by Murphy and Dolan. He was in direct competition with Murphy and Dolan who were beating him out of the government contracts with cattle stolen from his herds and sold at unmatchable prices.[17]

Chisum attempted to gain assistance from the army at Fort Stanton but the commanding officer, Captain George Purington, refused stating he had no authority to interfere in civil matters. He suggested Chisum take the issue before the sheriff of Lincoln County, William Brady. The sheriff, however, was no friend of Chisum. He aligned closely with Murphy having been old army buddies and heavily indebted to him and the Santa Fe Ring. Finding no help from Brady, Chisum took

CHAPTER 1: A BRIEF HISTORY | 13

*Figure 2. Lawrence Murphy
(Unknown photography studio.) Public domain.*

*Figure 3. James Dolan
(Unknown photography studio.) Public domain.*

matters into his own hands and decided to alleviate the loss of cattle from his herds. Shooting and killing occurred on both sides until reaching an uneasy truce. But at a cow camp near Seven Rivers, several thieves were arrested including the Kid. Initially believing he could earn good pay by protecting Chisum's herds, he wound up in a cellar under an adobe house in Lincoln used as the county jail.

The law eventually released Billy since charges of cattle theft could not be proven. There was some dispute about his activities after his release. Frank Coe said he came to his ranch in the Fall of 1877 and spent the winter with him. George Coe, Frank's cousin, said the Kid helped Billy Morton and Frank Baker drive some cattle to Lincoln, but they failed to pay him. He threatened to kill them both, and only the intervention by Jesse Evans prevented their deaths. It was a short time later, Dick Brewer, John Tunstall's foreman, hired the Kid.

Barbara Jones, who lived in Seven Rivers, refuted both these stories. She remarked that the Kid walked into her ranch after spending three days afoot nearly collapsing at her door. His story was that Apaches had jumped him and a friend near the top of the Guadalupe Mountains nearly thirty miles distant. His friend, James O'Keefe, was able to escape on his horse, but the Kid had to hide out after the Apaches stole his. Staying hidden during the day, he walked at night until he arrived at Jones's ranch. The Kid stayed there several days, helping around the house and playing with the children. He allegedly developed a strong bond with her son, John, during this time. As I intimated earlier, these stories are anecdotal and not proven facts. The disparity among the stories highlights the difficulty in learning which accounts, if any, are accurate. Still, each on its merit is interesting and plausible.[18]

While the Kid was traveling around Lincoln County, he received word through Jesse Evans that Sheriff Mariano

Barela threatened to kill the Kid if he didn't return the mare belonging to the sheriff's daughter. By now, the horse had changed hands several times. The horse was now in possession of Ellen Casey who was moving cattle she secretly removed from the Tunstall ranch. Tunstall and partner, Alexander McSween, loaned her a sum of money and took possession of her animals as collateral for the loan. Their arrangement was highly lucrative for them because if she could not pay the loan back, they would acquire ownership of the cattle at a cost substantially lower than market prices.

Ellen Casey believed she was the victim of a swindle and she was in the process of moving the cattle with more than a few others from the Tunstall ranch to Texas. The Kid crossed her path, seeing a mare he recognized as the one he stole from Sheriff Barela. Billy attempted to trade for the horse but was unable to reach an agreement with Casey. He allegedly explained to her that because Jesse Evans was in cahoots with Sheriff Barela, Evans would recognize the brand on the mare and make trouble for him. So, he traded the mare for the horse he was currently riding. The Kid then attempted to gain employment with the Casey group on their way across the Llano Estacado, Spanish for "Staked Plains," en route to Texas after leaving their ranch on the Hondo River. That didn't work out either. Ellen Casey believed the Kid would steal the mare and the other horses and leave them to walk to Texas. No offer of employment was forthcoming.[19]

In the meantime, Brewer and his Tunstall band caught up with Ellen Casey and her companion, Abner McCabe, along with the cattle she had taken from Tunstall's ranch. Brewer separated 209 head and drove them back to Tunstall's place on the Feliz River, leaving the remainder at a nearby cow camp. Ellen Casey returned to Seven Rivers and then back to her home on the Hondo River. Brewer returned to her spread later and arrested her sons, Will and Robert Case and transported them to Lincoln. At the request of Mrs. Casey, John Chisum intervened on her behalf and gained the release of Will and Robert. Once again, no documentation supports this account, but it indeed may have occurred. There was no further mention of the Kid until he appeared in Lincoln as winter began.[20]

Now using the name of Billy Bonney, he rode the grub line either on the Pecos River or at Chisum's South Spring ranch. Evans and company had been arrested on warrants for cattle rustling and were in the underground cells of the Lincoln County jail. But as it happened, the Boys were liberated from their confines during the night hours of Saturday, November 16, 1877. The rescue party consisted of Buck Morton, Billy Mathews, Dick Lloyd, Charlie Crawford and possibly, the Kid who was trying so desperately to get back in Jesse Evans's good graces. They headed to Charlie Bowdre's ranch on Eagle Creek and then on to Brewer's place where they ate breakfast and stole twelve of Brewer's horses. Crossing Tunstall's Feliz ranch, they eventually made their way to Seven Rivers.

The Kid still had possession of Tunstall's dapple-grey buggy team in Seven Rivers. At the request of Tunstall, the Sheriff, though it's uncertain which one—probably Dick Brewer—went to Seven Rivers, arrested the Kid and recovered the horses. After spending a brief sentence, the law again released the Kid because no one could prove he stole the horses. Brewer or Tunstall or both offered Billy a deal he couldn't refuse, and Billy began employment with Tunstall. It's important to note that Lily Casey, Ellen Casey's daughter recalled that Billy was about fifteen during the time he spent in the Lincoln County "dungeon."[21] She repeated the same information later several times, suggesting that Billy was even younger than initially suspected. It was winter of 1877, and if he were fifteen then, he would have been only twelve when his mother died and only nineteen at the time of his death in 1881. Though this adds more corroboration to his young age, verified documentation is still absent.

There continued much rancor and corruption throughout the remainder of 1877 and into the year 1878. Disputes between Governor Axtell's merry band of cutthroats inclusive of the Murphy-Dolan faction raged on against the Tunstall, McSween, and Chisum contingent who were not clean themselves. Meanwhile, Billy was spending his winter days with the likes of Dick Brewer, Fred Waite, Gottfried Gauss, neighboring rancher "Dutch" Martin Martz, and a former Indian agency teamster named Bill McCloskey. He was learning about honor, respect, and loyalty. The Kid spent all his spare time, gaining skill as a shootist; cleaning his weapons and practicing speed and accuracy at shooting. Absent other events interfering with his growing up, he might have progressed to become a highly productive member of society. Unfortunately, with the untimely death of his employer and mentor, John Tunstall, his positive social learning was soon to be abruptly curtailed.[22]

Billy grew as a person during this period. He gained friends quickly due to his glowing personality. They described him as intelligent and engaging, slightly built but quick and ambidextrous. He was only five feet seven with hazel-colored eyes and sandy blonde hair. He spoke Spanish fluently, and he was well thought of among the New Mexican population. His mother must have raised him well because his friends and associates knew him as courteous and gentlemanly. What separated Billy from other youth of his age was that he was eager to learn and was quick-minded. He learned early on that he did not have the physique to perform heavy labor and if he had to defend himself, he could not do so physically. His only savior was learning a great skill with both rifle and pistol as his means of defense. He offset despair with humor, and he met hatred with kindness. Never one to shirk his responsibilities, his ability to be dangerous during emergencies was matched with his superior planning abilities. He learned what it meant to place others above himself, and loyalty replaced avarice. However, the one thing he carried with him was his propensity for revenge; the Kid never buried that so deep it couldn't be reached when he felt it necessary.[23]

Death of John Tunstall

Many people believe he and Tunstall became friends, but this portrayal of their relationship may be inaccurate. While Billy admired Tunstall, there was never any written evidence through correspondence to the Tunstall family or otherwise that this close relationship existed. The only proof that Tunstall respected Billy lay in the fact that the Kid was always close by when Tunstall needed him. Was evidence required to prove their closeness? Not really. Actions speak louder than words, and it was apparent through Billy's efforts how much he admired Tunstall, and the reverse was also correct.[24]

There are numerous books written about the Lincoln County War, and the detail provided is both enlightening and thorough.[25] In so much as a complete description of facts before, during, and immediately after the war would be interesting, it is beyond the scope of this study. However, it may suffice to suggest that the combination of greed, corruption, and revenge were all crucial in fulminating the armed conflict and the Battle of Lincoln on July 14–19, 1878.[26] There were also specific instances that one may conclude directly contributed to the final shootout. The previous incidents I've described were not totally in and of themselves responsible for the resulting conflict. But they had a lot to do with it.

Alexander McSween and John Tunstall were considered interlopers in what was viewed as a well-oiled conspiracy to steal cattle to fulfill Indian and army contracts, increase land holdings through deceit and fraud and when all else failed, resort to murder. McSween and Tunstall had their own schemes brewing as well. Their combined intent was to accomplish the same outcome, but without the outright criminality practiced by the Murphy-Dolan bunch. When they found themselves boxed in by circumstances they could not control, McSween and Tunstall resorted to letter writing and the filing of complaints with persons they believed had the clout to protect them. In other words, they took a more civilized approach to remedy the lawlessness. The other side ignored constitutionality, and they had backing from Governor Axtell, corrupt lawmen, courts and officials. Bypassing legality, they used what-ever underhanded means available to them to run McSween and Tunstall out of business. When their efforts failed, they resorted to murder.[27]

It began first with the murder of John Tunstall at approximately 5:00 p.m. on February 18, 1878, who was shot in the chest and then in the back of the head by a posse of the Boys operating under the direction of Sheriff William Brady. The particulars of why this posse was rounding up Tunstall's horses and cattle while important, was less so than the killing itself. Already evident the detachment was acting maliciously; Tunstall's murder sparked a wildfire that resulted in rage and revenge. No one could interpret the act in any other way. It was a declaration of War. Billy Bonney was one who was most affected, but he wasn't the only one.[28]

After a brief coroner's inquest, the jury determined Jesse Evans, Frank Baker, Tom Hill, George Hindman, James Dolan, Billy Morton, and others not yet identified committed the murder. Justice of the Peace Wilson issued arrest warrants

Figure 4. John Henry Tunstall. Public domain.

for those involved in Tunstall's killing as well as one for Sheriff Brady based on a complaint lodged by Alexander McSween for theft. Wilson gave the arrest warrants to Constable Atanacio Martinez who out of self-preservation was uninterested in serving them. Eventually, Constable Martinez, accompanied by Fred Waite and the Kid went to the Dolan store to serve the warrants. Brady and his men met them with armed resistance. Brady refused to allow the arrest of anyone present and subsequently arrested the three. Martinez was ultimately released but not Waite and the Kid. The arrest prevented the Kid from attending Tunstall's funeral the following day, adding insult to injury.[29] Brady arrested those individuals because he could, not because he had a legal authority to do so. Sheriff Brady didn't realize it at the time, but his actions sealed his fate. He was going to die soon for his corrupt deeds.[30]

The Regulators

The back and forth of corruption continued throughout February and March. McSween was engaged in his letter-writing routine while Dick Brewer believed McSween's actions would prove ineffective. On March 1, 1878, Brewer appeared before Justice Wilson and was appointed a deputy constable. His compadres including John Middleton, Fred Waite, Doc Scurlock, Charlie Bowdre, John Smith, Frank McNab, Henry Brown, Jim French, and Billy Bonney were subsequently sworn in. Coining the name "Regulators," they swore to protect each other and hunt down Tunstall's murderers.[31]

Honorable intentions, maybe, but it was clear they all had a singular thought. Warrants provided them with the power of arrest. However, those arrested and handed over to Sheriff Brady would never see the inside of a jail. Execution, therefore, must have been their underlying intent.

Buck Morton, Frank Baker, and Dick Lloyd were the first to be captured near the Peñasco River on March 6, 1878, and were killed three days later while allegedly attempting to escape. When Brewer returned to Lincoln, he learned that Samuel B. Axtell issued a proclamation retroactively revoking the commissions of the Regulators effective the same day they killed Morton and Baker. As well, the declaration also removed Justice of the Peace Wilson from office. Governor Axtell's proclamation was probably illegal, but even if he didn't have the authority, he had the power. Regardless, Brewer and his Regulators were outlaws by gubernatorial decree. All responsibility for law and order was in the hands of Sheriff William Brady and his ruthless band. Judge Warren Bristol regulated all legal writs and processes. Thomas B. Catron and the Santa Fe Ring were firmly in control. Or so they thought.[32]

On April Fool's Day, April 1, 1878, Sheriff Brady took his

*Figure 5. Dick Brewer
(Unknown photographer.) Public domain.*

last breath. At about 9:30 a.m. Brady walked down the main street from Dolan's store toward the Tunstall store. The crowd he was with, deputies George Peppin, Billy Mathews, George Hindman, and Jack Long, had gotten ahead of him. As he caught up to them at a wooden gate at the corral near the eastern end of the store, the gate swung open, and he was slammed with a hail of lead, knocking him to the ground. Eventually, Brady fell dead in the street, Hindman was mortally wounded, and the remaining deputies ran for cover.[33]

*Figure 6. Sheriff William Brady
(Unknown photographer.) Public domain.*

As the street emptied, the Kid and Jim French ran out to recover a Winchester rifle Brady allegedly took from the Kid when he arrested him previously. There may have also been a piece of paper in Brady's vest of interest to Billy; possibly a court order for the arrest of Alexander McSween as he was expected to be in the company of army soldiers from Fort Stanton riding into Lincoln that morning.[34]

Billy Mathews fired on the two from a house down the street. The Kid was struck by Mathews's bullet, causing a flesh wound in his upper thigh. The round continued through French's leg resulting in severe damage. After reaching safety, five Regulators, Middleton, Brown, McNab, Waite, and the Kid barreled out of the corral on horseback and galloped away. French remained behind due to the severity of his wound, and Sam Corbet hid him under the floorboards of Corbet's house.[35]

Blazer's Mill

Regardless of the perspective one might have had, killing Sheriff Brady added gasoline to an already blazing flame. Someone clearly murdered Sheriff Brady. The Regulators had thrown down their gauntlets and chose to do battle with the flagrantly corrupt legal system. Their next stop was Blazer's Mill some three days later. Looking for "Buckshot Roberts" as a man whose name appeared on Tunstall's murderers' list, they ran headlong into him.

An ensuing gun battle left Roberts mortally wounded, and Dick Brewer shot through the head. Middleton, Scurlock, Coe and the Kid were only slightly injured.[36] The Regulators shot during the raucous engagement in Lincoln and Blazer's Mill retired to the Ruidoso area to recover. Dr. Ealy amputated Coe's trigger finger. Charlie Bowdre was laying sore and tender from the slug that bounced off his belt buckle. Jim French lay nursing the hole through his leg, and the Kid nursed the grazing wound on his arm. Middleton had been shot but not as severely as first believed.

They all laid low recuperating while events were progressing in Lincoln. The Kid had earned a reputation now as a fighting man and was equal to those he accompanied. Because he spoke fluent Spanish and knew their customs, he was liked by most he met.[37]

The Indictments

While the Regulators rested up, Judge William Bristol empaneled a grand jury on April 13, 1878. Indictments generated warrants for the arrest of those responsible for Tunstall's murder against Jesse Evans, George Davis, Manual Segovia, and John Long, naming Dolan and Mathews as accessories. The grand jury also indicted Middleton, Waite, Brown and the Kid under the name of Henry Antrim for the murder of Brady and Hindman as well as the murder of "Buckshot" Roberts. Included in the Roberts indictment were Charlie Bowdre, Doc Scurlock, Steve Stephens, John Scroggins, and George Coe. The grand jury also indicted Dolan and Riley for cattle theft, and Sheriff Brady's replacement, Acting Sheriff John Copeland, proceeded to enforce the grand jury warrants. The grand jury fully exonerated Alexander McSween of an embezzlement charge over an insurance claim, and after making bond, Dolan and Riley completed their business dealings and departed Lincoln with terminally ill, Lawrence Murphy.[38]

With Brewer dead, their commissions revoked, the Regulators were on the run. McNab was elected to captain the bunch and was moving his crew to the Seven Rivers, New Mexico area, home to many of the Tunstall murder posse. McSween had posted a reward on behalf of the Tunstall family for the apprehension and conviction of the murderers of John Tunstall. In the meantime, the Department of Justice was sending a special agent to investigate Tunstall's murder in addition to the alleged criminal activities of local federal officials. A Department of Interior inspector was also en route to examine Indian agency contracts and Dolan's involvement with the Lincoln Post Office. Peppin, Mathews, and Hurley spurred the Seven Rivers group into action when they closely linked McSween and John Chisum in interests contrary to the settlers of Seven Rivers. About thirty of the self-appointed posse headed to Lincoln to help Sheriff Copeland arrest the murderers of Brady, Hindman, Morton, and Baker. Their targets were Middleton, Waite, Bowdre and the Kid.[39]

Figure 7. Charlie Bowdre (Unknown studio photographer.) Public domain.

Battle of Fritz Ranch

Frank McNab was leading his group of Regulators into an ambush, but he didn't know it. Running into a wall of lead, McNab died instantly and James A. "AB" Saunders, shot in the hip, was left to lay where he fell. Frank Coe eventually surrendered, but they later released him originally thinking he was the Kid but learning otherwise. The Seven Rivers posse headed for Lincoln and on May 1, 1878, they waited at the Ellis corrals to ambush the McSween party, but no one was there. George Coe, thinking Frank McNab was dead, had climbed to the roof of the Ellis house with Henry Brown and began shooting at the posse. "Dutch" Charlie Kruling was shot in the legs by Coe, and six others were down. The battle raged throughout the day, but eventually, Sheriff Copeland and an army troop were able to intervene in the fighting. In all the confusion, Frank Coe, who was thought dead but merely captured, was able to slip away and rejoin his friends.[40]

After McNab's burial next to Tunstall's grave, McSween went before a Justice of the Peace in San Patricio and swore complaints against members of the Seven Rivers posse.[41] Sheriff Copeland, with the help of Colonel Nathan Dudley from Fort Stanton, arrested the whole Seven Rivers crowd. Col. Dudley who was Murphy-Dolan friendly later released the group and ordered Lieutenants Goodwin and Smith to escort Copeland to San Patricio to arrest McSween, John Windenmann, and others for rioting. Everyone was arresting everyone. The Seven Rivers crowd were bound over for trial, and they all returned to Fort Stanton. Upon arriving at the fort, Dudley placed the McSween group in the guardhouse but left the Seven Rivers men free to roam the fort. David Easton, the Lincoln Justice of the Peace who was to hear the case against the McSween contingent resigned, and Dudley found himself holding the bag. He back peddled on Sheriff Copeland and dumped the mess back in his lap. With no military support, Copeland released everyone.[42]

Taking on a New Enemy

Doc Scurlock, who had been appointed a deputy by Sheriff Copeland, took command of the Regulators and led them to a Dolan-Riley cow camp on the Black River where they caught up with Frank McNab's killers. They recovered several horses belonging to McNab, Saunders, and Tunstall, leaving two outlaws wounded and one dead. This action precipitated a period of calm while Department of Justice agent, Frank Warner Angel, took depositions and investigated Tunstall's

Figure 8. Thomas B. Catron (Anonymous.) Public domain.

murder. However, the Regulators made a mistake when they attacked the Black River cow camp. Dolan and Riley were no longer the owners; the cow camp now belonged to Thomas B. Catron. It gave Catron the perfect opportunity to petition the governor asking for intervention. Governor Axtell issued a proclamation removing Copeland as sheriff and appointing the Ring's sycophant, George Peppin in his place. Peppin, a Dolan man, pursued McSween and the Regulators with the intent of arresting or killing the remaining members. The chase went on throughout June, and much of July until the two sides clashed in Lincoln on July 15, 1878.[43]

The Regulators were running for their lives with Peppin's

deputies ready to shoot them on sight. By now the Kid had rejoined the group after spending time on the Chisum ranch. As time crawled toward the ultimate battle, skirmishes occurred around San Patricio. Sheriff Peppin ransacked the village and threatened the villagers to the extent they were afraid to provide the Regulators with any assistance. The members took sanctuary once again at the Chisum ranch, out of reach of the Peppin band.

Battle of Lincoln

Hearing that the President was about to remove the Indian agent, the governor, and the United States Attorney from office as a result of their corruption, McSween and the Regulators returned to Lincoln on July 14, 1878. Now reinforced by native New Mexicans, the Regulators consisting of approximately sixty men, occupied Lincoln. They far outnumbered Peppin's men. The Kid and about a dozen others guarded McSween in his home while the others took positions throughout the town. The shooting began the next day when a posse of men who had been searching for the McSween men, rode into town hell-bent on rescuing their compatriots.[44]

The Kid, now a full-fledged warrior in his own right, led his Regulators unscathed to shelter. For the better part of five days, they battled with the Peppin bunch. Sheriff Peppin even petitioned Col. Dudley for the use of one of his howitzers, but due to a recent law passed by Congress called the *Posse Comitatus Act*, Dudley was constrained and refused the request. He sent a soldier with a message in response to Peppin, but someone shot at him upon entering Lincoln. Shooting at the soldier along with his friend Dolan's request for assistance ultimately justified Dudley to send troops for the "protection of innocent women and children of Lincoln." After a brief meeting with his officers, Dudley ordered Captain

George Purington to lead a column consisting of four officers, a company of cavalry and another of infantry. That sounds like a sizeable contingent, but only thirty-five troopers were involved. It was the addition of a twelve-pound howitzer and a Gatling gun that evened the playing field. Due to their positioning, none of the McSween supporters could fire in the direction of Peppin's forces without hitting a soldier. McSween's house was now isolated.[45]

The details of the battle are well-documented in numerous texts, and no doubt, the maneuverings of both sides are fascinating to study. For this book, only the outcome is relevant. Even though Susan McSween implored Col. Dudley to intervene and stop the bloodshed, he refused to do so, still supporting Peppin's bunch. Ultimately, McSween's house was set afire, and her husband killed. The Kid and four others, Chávez y Chávez, Harvey Morris, Jim French, and Tom O'Folliard, attempted to escape. Morris didn't make it and was the first to fall, shot at the gate. McSween died outside the house. Susan McSween was able to walk away, but for sure, she would make miserable the lives of her husband's killers.[46]

On to Fort Sumner

The Kid and his small band made their escape while several people including Alexander McSween lay dead in the street. The battle, now over, reduced the Regulators to a group of nineteen men including the Kid, Tom O'Folliard, Steve Stephens, the Coes, Doc Scurlock, Charlie Bowdre, Henry Brown, Jim French, John Middleton, John Scroggins, Fernando Herrera, Ignacio Gonzales, and Atanacio Martinez. Making their way to Fort Sumner using the passage through the Chisum ranch, no one from Lincoln County pursued them. George Peppin resigned as Sheriff and became a Fort Stanton butcher. Scurlock and Charlie Bowdre went to work for Pete Maxwell in Fort Sumner, and the remainder including the Kid headed for Puerto de Luna, a haven for stolen horses. Trouble was lurking, however, because Sheriff Desiderio Romero of San Miguel County was asking questions about Billy and his bunch.⁴⁷

Billy and his bunch decided to confront Sheriff Romero and his party. In a head-to-head conversation, Romero admitted he had no warrants for the group. Shortly after that, Romero and his posse departed the area without incident. Remaining in the Anton Chico area, Billy returned to what interested him the most. He partied and danced with the young ladies. But revenge still burned within him. By now Chisum had deserted him, and Tunstall's holdings were gone. Nothing left for Billy Bonney and his Regulators but cattle rustling, they stole cattle where they could and disposed of them as needed. Their survival relied on a cash and carry basis. At one point, they even returned to Lincoln and took over the town. After stealing more livestock, they moved them to Tascosa, Texas, where the Kid's group sold them with no questions asked.⁴⁸

A New Governor

By this time, Lew Wallace had taken over the job as governor of the New Mexico Territory.⁴⁹ Mostly, civil order was in place in Lincoln County. Wallace declared an amnesty for which he pardoned all crimes committed between February 1, 1878, and the date of the proclamation. Great news for everyone except the Kid and the Regulators, there must have been a sign up somewhere for the Regulators, "Does Not Apply!" Billy ignored the proclamation. He, Tom O'Folliard, Doc Scurlock and Jim French returned to Lincoln and attempted to make peace with Dolan and Evans on the anniversary of Tunstall's death. Thinking they had reached an agreement, Billy and his crew were engaging in celebration when he became an eyewitness to the murder of Susan McSween's attorney, Huston Chapman. Shot dead in the street by Jesse Evans and William Campbell, Billy was now in danger of being named an accomplice to another murder.[50]

Figure 9. Governor Lew Wallace
(Unknown photographer.) Public domain.

Governor Wallace traveled to Lincoln to view firsthand the lawlessness of the region. While he was there, he drew up a list of some thirty-five names. Organizing a militia called the Lincoln County Rifles led by Juan Patrón and assisted by the cavalry, their first act was to capture Evans, Campbell, and Dolan and thirty-two others. It was then Wallace received a letter from an unsuspecting source, Billy Bonney, willing to become a witness to the killing of Huston Chapman. Wallace and the Kid agreed that they would meet at Squire Wilson's house on March 15, 1879, whereby Wallace offered exemption from prosecution for Billy to testify against Dolan, Evans, and Campbell. Billy met with Wallace and provided him with a rundown of what he knew.[51] Whether or not Wallace intended to exempt Billy for his crimes is unknown, but Billy did ultimately testify as agreed and provided additional testimony to Col. Dudley's court of inquiry. A grand jury returned nearly two hundred indictments against the men who had opposed the Tunstall-McSween regime, but Col. Dudley was exonerated.[52]

No pardon came from Wallace and Billy was left to languish in Juan Patrón's store, doubling as Billy's jail. He knew U.S. Marshal John Sherman and his deputy were on their way to Fort Stanton to escort him to La Mesilla to stand trial in federal court for the murder of "Buckshot" Roberts. Even if he avoided that trial, the Santa Fe Ring would still prosecute him for the killing of William Brady. He had no choice except to walk out of his prison, and with Tom O'Folliard, escape to Fort Sumner.

The Kid's Survival

Back and forth to Lincoln several times, Billy avoided capture by both the army and newly appointed Sheriff George Kimbrell. For the most part, he made his home in Fort Sumner. While the law was still after him, the Kid knew if they caught him, he would be subjected to a "reasonably" fair trial and then hung. Following the path of least resistance, he returned to the one method at which he was an expert. Rustling cattle from the big ranches on the Llano Estacado was a lucrative business. Now he was accompanied by Dave Rudabaugh, Tom Pickett and Billy Wilson. Rudabaugh and Pickett were former Las Vegas policemen, but "Dirty Dave" as called himself was a miserable thug who delighted in train robberies and stagecoach holdups while under the protection of a crooked city marshal, John Joshua Web. When the law finally arrested

Web, Rudabaugh tried to break him out and, in the process, killed the jailer, Lino Valdez. Pickett, a former Texas Ranger, was nearly as wicked as "Dirty Dave." For the most part, they stayed out of sight by working as cowboys at the Yerby ranch. They augmented their income by riding with Charlie Bowdre and the Kid. The downside was that while Billy and his partners were working eastern New Mexico, cattle predation was occurring elsewhere as well. Ranchers suffered considerable losses, and they blamed the Kid for convenience and revenge.[53]

The Kid had become very vocal about his disgust with John Chisum for failing to pay him for fighting for Alexander McSween and Chisum during the Lincoln County War. He accosted Chisum in Fort Sumner at one point and threatened to kill the "Old Man" if he didn't pay up. Chisum refused to pay Billy saying he never promised such a thing. Figuring he didn't need further grief, he let the Chisum go and instead turned to steal more of Chisum's cattle to reimburse himself in kind from Chisum's herd.[54]

Death of "Texas Red"

Jim Chisum, John Chisum's brother, had been looking for rebranded Chisum stock near Fort Sumner when Billy and his companions rode into their camp. After a brief encounter, Billy invited the Chisum band to the fort for some drinks. When they arrived at Bob Hargrove's saloon, a man named "Texas Red" Joe Grant was generally making himself a nuisance and was obnoxiously drunk. Grant bet Billy $25 that he could kill a man before the Kid could. Grant pulled an ivory-handled pistol out of a holster belonging to Jack Finan and replaced it with his own. Billy went to Grant pretending to admire Grant's new firearm. Billy was aware that Finan had previously fired three shots from that same gun and had not reloaded. Joe Grant allowed Billy to inspect the piece and as Billy did so, he spun the cylinder so that the next time it was cocked the hammer would fall on an empty cartridge and gave it back to Grant.[55]

Grant became more violent as the night went on and eventually turned towards Jim Chisum and said he was going to kill John Chisum. Billy advised him he had the wrong man and said the man was John's brother. Grant called Billy a liar and squared off at him. When he drew and fired his revolver, all he heard was the click of an empty chamber followed by three quick retorts of Billy's gun. Grant slammed into the floor like a sack of flour. Billy later remarked to Postmaster Milnor Rudolf when asked what happened, said, "It was a game of two, and I got there first."[56]

Stinking Springs

Cattle rustling continued in the Lincoln, and San Miguel counties and ranchers were tired of their losses to the likes of Billy the Kid and his gang. In an attempt to curtail rustling activities, John Chisum and several other ranchers enticed a tall, Texas implant from Roswell, New Mexico, to run for sheriff of Lincoln County. His name was Patrick Floyd Garrett. Garrett was familiar with Fort Sumner and at one time worked for Pete Maxwell on his ranch. Garrett and Bonney were friends, and to some extent, they shared the outlaw trail. Chisum decided Garrett was the perfect man to go after the Kid.

Garrett was elected sheriff of Lincoln County, but since he didn't take office until the following January, Sheriff Kimbrell appointed him as a deputy. At about the same time, the U.S. Secret Service was also interested in the Kid for involvement in counterfeiting. Special Agent Azariah Wild was sent to discover the source and make-up of the counterfeiting ring, and he needed help. He asked U.S. Marshal John Sherman to

*Figure 10. Patrick Floyd Garrett
(Unknown photographer.) Public domain.*

send him a commission in the name of John Hurley. Instead, Sherman sent two in that name. Wild crossed out the name on one of the commissions and placed Garrett's name on the document. He probably had no authority to do so, and now Garrett was also commissioned a deputy U.S. Marshal.[57]

The Kid and his group of Dave Rudabaugh, Joe Cook, Billy Wilson, and Buck Edwards stole several horses in White Oaks and stopped over at the Greathouse Trading Post to replenish and rest. Constable Thomas B. Longworth raised a posse to pursue the kid and his gang and surrounded the trading post on November 27, 1880. Leaving the detachment to get reinforcements and more supplies, the constable left Jim Carlyle in charge. Trying to talk the Kid and the rest into surrendering, Carlyle entered the establishment and tried to negotiate with the Kid. Probably by mistake, someone fired a shot that touched off a battle where bullets were flying in both directions. The Kid and his gang eventually made their escape. Unfortunately, someone killed Jim Carlyle in the melee.

Billy and company made their way to Anton Chico as Wild's posse was leaving Roswell. Deputy U.S. Marshals Bob Olinger and Pat Garrett led the lawmen out of Roswell, and they caught one of the Kid's gang members on the way, Joseph Cook. Continuing, they located and arrested two more men, John Joshua Webb, and George Davis, both escapees from the Las Vegas jail. The posse was moving North along the Pecos River and gathering up outlaws as they went. Meanwhile, Governor Lew Wallace posted a reward of $500 for Billy's arrest adding to the Kid's troubles. Now everyone was looking for him.[58]

Garrett received word that the Kid and his gang were, by this time, in Fort Sumner. Calling for the rest of his posse to join him, they rode into Fort Sumner and took up positions. Someone in town alerted Billy before Garrett's arrival, and he and his boys escaped the trap. It was cold, snowing and in general just all-around lousy weather. Garrett lured Billy back to Fort Sumner by sending a Fort Sumner resident to Billy's hideout to tell him Garrett and the posse returned to White Oaks. About eleven o'clock that night, the Kid and his gang rode into town. He and his men rode into an ambush. All but Tom O'Folliard made their escape once more. O'Folliard, however, was shot in the chest and after languishing for several hours, later died of his wound.

Familiar with the area, Garrett knew Billy would head for an old forage station at Stinking Springs. After making their way to the stone building in which the gang was hiding, Garrett and his posse surrounded the place. Expecting Billy to

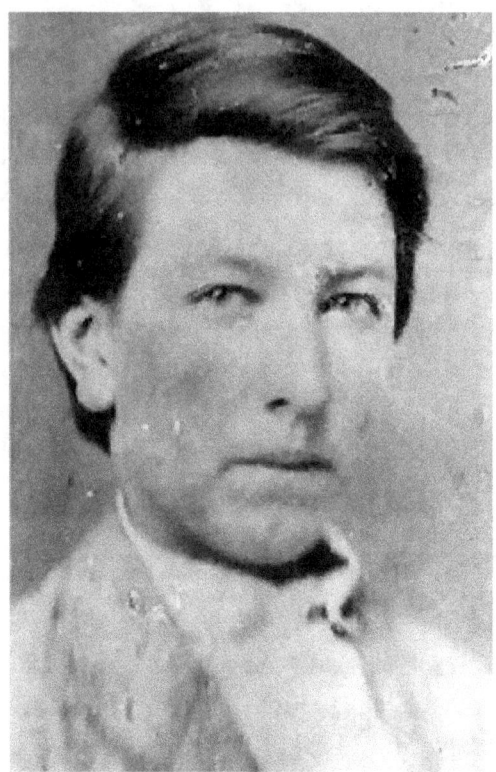

*Figure 11. Tom O'Folliard
(Unknown photographer.) Public domain.*

come out and feed the horses the next morning, a man wearing a Mexican sombrero exited the building.

The Sheriff and his men fired at him, believing he was the Kid. As it turned out, the man was Charlie Bowdre, and they shot him three times. A case of mistaken identity caused his death.

Anticipating Billy's attempt to escape, Garrett shot one of the horses, and it fell into the doorway of the rock house. The dead horse blocked their exit, and the Kid eventually surrendered. The gang was taken into custody and transported back to Fort Sumner on Christmas Eve, 1880.[59]

The Trial

Billy finally found himself sitting in the Santa Fe jail awaiting transport to La Mesilla to stand trial for the murder of William Brady. Two of his close friends Charlie Bowdre and Tom O'Folliard were now dead, and the remainder of his gang was in custody. From his confines, he authored his last three letters to Governor Wallace asking the Governor to honor his promise of a pardon. The letters went unanswered, and deputies transported Billy to La Mesilla on March 28, 1880.[60]

Brought before Judge Warren Bristol in La Mesilla, Bristol's court tried Billy for several crimes including the deaths of Buckshot" Roberts and Sheriff William Brady. His attorney, Ira Leonard, was able to have several charges dismissed but Billy couldn't avoid the trial for the murder of Sheriff Brady. In a sham trial conducted by Judge Bristol, an acolyte of the Ring, Judge Bristol delivered the instructions to the jury comprised of non-English speaking members. In a sense, the Judge sealed Billy's fate by taking away any presumption of innocence. Billy was convicted and sentenced to hang in Lincoln on the 13th day of May 1881.[61]

Billy, heavily shackled, and his guards made their way to Fort Stanton. Deputy Robert Olinger and Sheriff Pat Garrett escorted him the remainder of the way to Lincoln. Since Lincoln had no jail of sorts, Garrett and Olinger took Billy to the old Dolan store now serving as Lincoln's courthouse. There he was to remain until the date of his sentence to be carried out. Garrett chose Bob Olinger and J. W. Bell to guard him.[62]

The Escape

Sitting uncomfortably chained to the floor; Billy awaited his fate. Deputy Bell supposedly treated him with courtesy. However, Olinger was a bully. Continually threatening the Kid and

*Figure 12. Samuel B. Axtell
(Unknown photographer.) Public domain.*

abusing him, the rage inside Billy against Olinger increased. Always looking for means to escape, Billy bided his time. Garrett warned Bell and Olinger to be careful of the Kid. He knew Billy and understood the Kid would exploit any mistake made by either of the deputies. Despite the treatment by Olinger, Billy kept a positive outlook, for somehow he knew there would be no hangman's noose for him.[63]

By April 28th, the Kid and the deputies settled into their routines. Each day food was sent at about noon to the jail from the Wortley Hotel. Then at supper time, Olinger escorted the prisoners to the Wortley for their evening meal. Billy remained on the second floor of the makeshift courthouse alone with Deputy Bell to eat alone. Billy finally saw his chance and grabbed a pistol. Whether he retrieved it from Bell or some other means, no one knows, but somehow Billy mortally wounded Bell. Lots of stories abound, but the fact is the Kid killed Bell regardless of how Billy obtained the pistol. Billy later reflected he had no intention to kill Bell as the deputy treated him well. The Kid grabbed Olinger's shotgun, which Olinger leaned against the wall before taking the other prisoners to supper. Billy patiently awaited Olinger to come running from the hotel.[64] Billy would now use the same gun Olinger threatened him with so many times when Olinger said he hoped the Kid would try to escape so he could shoot him in the back.

Olinger heard the gunshot and expected that Bell had shot Billy while trying to escape. There were a lot of things Olinger should have done before approaching the courthouse and running headlong into the kill zone was not one of them. Billy was waiting for him from the second-floor open window. Billy aimed the shotgun directly at Olinger's chest and greeted Olinger. "Hello, Bob," he said and then pulled both triggers. At a range of about ten feet, Olinger received the full force of lead pellets in his face and chest. In law enforcement, we call that "*DRT*," dead right there!" No better description for Olinger.[65]

Billy gathered up a Winchester and two pistols from the armory and ran to the balcony. There he told the townsfolk he didn't want to kill anyone else, but he would do so if they interfered with him leaving. Regardless of what account one might read, Billy made his way out of Lincoln and traveled to Fort Sumner. He ignored the advice from his friends to get out of the country and head for Mexico. He wasn't having any of that because he still had scores to settle. Billy may have intentionally used reverse psychology on Sheriff Garrett, knowing Garrett would never expect to find him in Fort Sumner because it seemed too obvious for him to be there. Or he just went to a location where he felt secure and was most comfortable. Either way, he ended up hiding almost in the open, where it seemed everyone, except his pursuers, believed him to be.[66]

*Figure 13. Robert Olinger
(Unknown photographer.) Public domain.*

The Final Shot

Over the next few weeks, Billy hid out in and around Fort Sumner. Even though several people had seen him, Sheriff

Garrett refused to believe the reports he received. Garrett could not believe Billy would so brazenly remain in New Mexico. Garrett put out feelers and sent a letter to one of his past posse men in Taiban, Manuel Brazil, asking him if he saw the Kid. Brazil responded that he knew Billy was around the area but was uncertain of the Kid's exact whereabouts. Garrett proposed a meeting with Brazil near Arroyo Taiban during the hours of darkness on July 13th.[67]

Garrett received word from his new deputy, John Poe, that while Poe was in White Oaks investigating more cattle rustling, he learned the Kid was in the Fort Sumner area. With Poe's story and Brazil's hunch, Garrett decided to ride to Fort Sumner. On the way to Billy's hideout, he stopped at Roswell and another deputy, "Kip" McKinney, joined the group. The three lawmen reached Taiban Creek on the night of July 13th, but Brazil failed to show. They agreed that since Poe was unknown in Fort Sumner, he would reconnoiter the area and determine Billy's location.[68] By then, someone warned the Kid that the Garrett posse was looking for him, but he didn't seem worried.

In contrast, Garrett had no confidence in the information he received and didn't believe Billy was in the area. However, Garrett knew that if Billy was around, there were several residences where he might be seen entering or exiting. One of them was the home of Paulita Maxwell, the sister of Pete Maxwell. There were numerous rumors that Paulita was pregnant with Billy's child. However, none were ever proven to be true.

Poe and McKinney knew no one in Fort Sumner, so they were of little help in recognizing the Kid. Allegedly Garrett believed their efforts were fruitless but eventually decided to talk with the one person he figured might know the whereabouts of the Kid, Pete Maxwell.[69]

Earlier, they allegedly saw a man get up off the ground in a nearby orchard. He was wearing a broad-brimmed hat, but he was too distant to recognize. They were to learn later it was the Kid, staying with Garrett's sister-in-law, Celsa Gutierrez. Exercising little precaution, if any, he posted Poe and McKinney near Maxwell's porch and entered Maxwell's house and then his room. According to some accounts, Celsa was cooking dinner for the Kid, and he wanted meat. She told him Maxwell had butchered a cow and it was hanging on Maxwell's porch. Billy picked up a butcher knife and went to slice off a slab of meat.[70]

Poe and McKinney saw him as he approached, supposedly only partially dressed, bareheaded and barefooted. When he saw Poe, the Kid drew his pistol and called out to him, "Quien es?" Moving into the room Garrett had just entered, the Kid addressed Maxwell asking him who it was beside his bed. Garrett supposedly recognized Billy, drew his gun and fired. He then dived to the side and fired again. Garrett scrambled to his feet and ran out the door, just barely in time to stop the two deputies from shooting Maxwell as he also left the room.[71]

The first bullet from Garrett's gun hit Billy just above the heart and dropped him. Never recovering from the wound, he laid there and died. The events of this night would be forever challenged; too many questions and not enough answers. Issues about the identity of the corpse, the manner, and the outcome of coroner's inquest, the configuration of the death scene and the hurried burial were never factually resolved. Regardless, it all boils down to one question, was Billy the Kid killed that night by Sheriff Pat Garrett or did Garrett kill the wrong man. Irrespective of whether Billy survived that night, the speculation that he did, true or not, created the foundation for others to claim his identity later.[72]

Numerous authors have chronicled historical information

emerging from the life of Billy the Kid, and many texts provide in-depth details for any curious reader. As I initially stated, I offered this chapter as a frame of reference, a snapshot of Billy's life, to assist the reader in gaining some perspective about William H. Bonney's environment. Was I to write a comprehensive study of all the events that transpired from birth to death of Billy the Kid, the product would result in thousands of pages, more than I intended for this book.

In a sense, that's what makes his life so interesting. His legend isn't just about him but also about everyone who ever knew him. I have provided "cliff notes," so the reader has a starting point and an ending point. I hope it is beneficial to your perception of Billy the Kid and assists you in your final evaluation of his life and his persona.

---

[1] Nolan, Frederick W. *The West of Billy the Kid.* University of Oklahoma Press,, 1998. (pp. 22-25)

[2] Rasch, Philip J. *Trailing Billy the Kid.* 1st edition, Western Publications, 1995.(pp. 23-35)

[3] Wallis, Michael. *Billy the Kid: The Endless Ride.* W. W. Norton and Company, 2007. (pp. 244-245).

[4] Nolan, Frederick W. "The Life and Death of John Henry Tunstall." Sunstone Press, 2009. (p.8)

[5] ---. *The West of Billy the Kid.* University of Oklahoma Press,, 1998. (pp. 22-25)

[6] Ibid.(p. 41)

[7] Ibid. (p. 28)

[8] Wallis, Michael. *Billy the Kid: The Endless Ride.* W. W. Norton and Company, 2007. (pp. 94-95)

[9] Utley, Robert Marshall. *Billy the Kid : A Short and Violent Life.* University of Nebraska Press, 1989. (pp. 10-16)

[10] Wallis, Michael. *Billy the Kid: The Endless Ride.* W. W. Norton and Company, 2007. (pp. 110-111).

[11] Nolan, Frederick W. *The West of Billy the Kid.* University of Oklahoma Press,, 1998. (p. 101)

[12] Ibid. (pp. 103-111)

[13] Ibid. (p. 103)

[14] Ibid. (p. 111-112)

[15] Ibid. (p. 112)

[16] Utley, Robert Marshall. *Billy the Kid : A Short and Violent Life.* University of Nebraska Press, 1989. (p. 46)

[17] Nolan, Frederick W. "The Life and Death of John Henry Tunstall." Sunstone Press, 2009. (pp. 188-190)

[18] ---. *The West of Billy the Kid.* University of Oklahoma Press,, 1998. (pp. 122-125)

[19] Ibid. (pp. 130-132)

[20] Ibid. (p. 132)

[21] Ibid. (p. 136)

[22] Ibid. (p. 141)

[23] Ibid. (pp. 135-154)

[24] Ibid. (p. 145)

[25] Nolan, Frederick W. "The Life and Death of John Henry Tunstall." Sunstone Press, 2009. (188-190)

26 ---. *The West of Billy the Kid.* University of Oklahoma Press,, 1998. (pp. 147-150)

27 ---. "The Life and Death of John Henry Tunstall." Sunstone Press, 2009. (pp.188-190)

28 ---. *The Lincoln County War: A Documentary History.* Sunstone Press, 1992. (p. 21)

29 ---. *The West of Billy the Kid.* University of Oklahoma Press,, 1998. (pp. 166-169)

30 Ibid. (p. 170)

31 Wallis, Michael. *Billy the Kid: The Endless Ride.* W. W. Norton and Company, 2007. (p. 199)

32 Nolan, Frederick W. *The West of Billy the Kid.* University of Oklahoma Press,, 1998. (p. 174)

33 Ibid. (p. 115)

34 Nolan, Frederick W. "The Life and Death of John Henry Tunstall." Sunstone Press, 2009. (p. 249)

35 ---. *The West of Billy the Kid.* University of Oklahoma Press,, 1998. (p. 188)

36 Caldwell, C. R. *Dead Right: The Lincoln County War.* Lulu.com, 2010. (pp. 131-142)

37 Rickards, Colin W. *The Gunfight at Blazer's Mill. Southwestern Studies Monograph.* Western Press, 1974. (pp. 36-37)

38 Nolan, Frederick W. *The West of Billy the Kid.* University of Oklahoma Press,, 1998. (pp. 211-212)

39 Ibid. (p. 212)

40 Caldwell, C. R. *Dead Right: The Lincoln County War.* Lulu.com, 2010. (pp. 143-146)

[41] Nolan, Frederick W. *The West of Billy the Kid.* University of Oklahoma Press,, 1998. (p. 220)

[42] Ibid. (pp. 215-222)

[43] Ibid. (pp. 224-225)

[44] Nolan, Frederick W. "The Life and Death of John Henry Tunstall." Sunstone Press, 2009. (pp. 304-322)

[45] Ibid. (pp. 304-322)

[46] Nolan, Frederick W. *The West of Billy the Kid.* University of Oklahoma Press,, 1998. (p. 162)

[47] ---. "The Life and Death of John Henry Tunstall." Sunstone Press, 2009. (p. 426)

[48] Chamberlain, Kathleen. *In the Shadow of Billy the Kid: Susan Mcsween and the Linclon County War.* University of New Mexico Press, 2013. (pp. 144-173)

[49] Boomhower, Ray E. *The Sword and the Pen.* Indiana Historical Society, 2005. (pp. 97-101)

[50] Nolan, Frederick W. *The West of Billy the Kid.* University of Oklahoma Press,, 1998. (p. 280)

[51] Utley, Robert Marshall. *Billy the Kid : A Short and Violent Life.* University of Nebraska Press, 1989. (p. 118)

[52] Boomhower, Ray E. *The Sword and the Pen.* Indiana Historical Society, 2005. (p. 118)

[53] Nolan, Frederick W. *The West of Billy the Kid.* University of Oklahoma Press,, 1998. (p. 326)

[54] Ibid. (p. 333)

[55] Ibid. (p. 335)

[56] Ibid. (p. 336)

[57] Ibid. (pp. 352-357)

[58] Ibid. (pp. 357-364)

[59] Utley, Robert Marshall. *Billy the Kid: A Short and Violent Life.* University of Nebraska Press, 1989. (pp. 158-159)

[60] Wallis, Michael. *Billy the Kid: The Endless Ride.* W. W. Norton and Company, 2007. (pp. 240-241)

[61] Ibid. (p. 242)

[62] Nolan, Frederick W. *The West of Billy the Kid.* University of Oklahoma Press,, 1998. (p. 403)

[63] Ibid. (p. 407)

[64] Utley, Robert Marshall. *Billy the Kid: A Short and Violent Life.* University of Nebraska Press, 1989. (p. 181)

[65] Ibid. (p. 187)

[66] Wallis, Michael. *Billy the Kid: The Endless Ride.* W. W. Norton and Company, 2007. (pp. 243-244)

[67] Nolan, Frederick W. *The West of Billy the Kid.* University of Oklahoma Press,, 1998. (p. 417)

[68] Ibid. (p. 418)

[69] Wallis, Michael. *Billy the Kid: The Endless Ride.* W. W. Norton and Company, 2007. (pp. 245-246)

[70] Ibid. (p. 247)

[71] Ibid. (p. 247)

[72] Nolan, Frederick W. *The West of Billy the Kid.* University of Oklahoma Press,, 1998. (pp. 426-429)

CHAPTER 2

An Unproven Death

FOR NOW, CONSIDER THE most significant event that remains unresolved for so many readers. Was Billy the Kid killed on July 14, 1881, and was he buried in the old Fort Sumner cemetery as purported by Pat Garrett in his book, *The Authentic Life of Billy the Kid?*[1]

Was there a vast conspiracy to protect Billy to allow him to live out his life, and avoid the hangman's noose? A significant number of people think so, and being lovers of conspiracy theories, they will produce volumes of information in support of Billy's survival. In contrast, the names of historical researchers and authors are just as numerous and adamant that Pat Garrett killed him that night, and any thought otherwise is absurd.

The suspicion that Billy survived opened a door for those who claimed to be him. The effort to further his legend was enthusiastic. If he died that night, in 1881, there was finality, and the door slammed shut. The only thing to discuss further is the likely undiscoverable tidbits of information concerning his origin from birth through about 1873.

For the sake of argument, consider those factors which might lead someone to conclude that Pat Garrett did not kill the Kid in Fort Sumner. In his book *Billy the Kid: Investigating*

History's Mysteries, W.C. Jameson describes in detail, discrepancies identified in the reported death of the Kid on July 14, 1881.[2] Jameson relies heavily on the investigative work conducted by Steve Sederwall who was acting in a quasi-official capacity with the Lincoln County Sheriff Department from approximately 2003 to 2007. During that time, Sederwall conducted both a crime scene examination and a detailed review of historical records from that era. Sederwall was a career law enforcement officer and a superior investigator known and admired by many for his superb investigative skills and imagination in solving crimes.

Sederwall identified significant discrepancies that both directly and indirectly controverted the historical representations made by many authors and historians. For a detailed description of the differences, Jameson's book documented Sederwall's explanations. However, some are worth further examination:

- After Garrett, Poe, and McKinney arrived at Pete Maxwell's house, Garrett stated he, ". . . stepped onto the porch and entered Maxwell's room through the open door." Because of National Archives record of the floorplan, it is obvious that Maxwell's room was 10 feet down the hallway after entering the hallway through a door on the porch. After walking down the hallway, Garrett would have had to turn left into Maxwell's room.[3]

A lot of detail was left out from Garrett's and Poe's account. But does that mean both officers lied, or does it only signify, they chose not to be specific in their sequence of events? Here's a clue. Storytellers select what they include in their accounts of an incident depending on what they consider relevant. Garrett and Poe may have omitted details because neither of them thought this information was important. It doesn't mean they were lying; only that they were not very thorough.

- In "The Bundy Avants Story," published in 1978, Avants described a meeting he had with Peter Maxwell years after the shooting. Maxwell allegedly told Avants, Billy the Kid was not shot by Garrett and Deputy Poe was not present.[4]

This story may have been true, but there are alternative questions. Did Maxwell's statement have a motive behind it? Was he protecting the legend or confiding in a friend? And when he said Poe was not present, did he mean in the room, at the house or Fort Sumner in general? Some crucial information is absent from this statement—primarily context.

- Maxwell's statement to Avants that Garrett was, "... pretty well shook up, as he didn't want it said that he had killed the wrong man." Maxwell said that Garrett killed a Mexican and that he promised Garrett he would keep quiet about the mistake.[5]

First, I would expect the thought of being, "pretty well shook up," would apply to anyone not sociopathic who killed a person, primarily if they viewed their life in danger at that moment. And secondly, since Garrett personally knew the Kid, this might load an additional weight on his psyche. One would have to question the relevance of this statement. Garrett might well have killed the wrong person, but this statement taken by itself doesn't lend much to Maxwell's account.

Next, I believe Maxwell didn't necessarily like Garrett and was somewhat fearful of him. Telling this story might be a way of getting back at Garrett. It would undoubtedly tarnish Garrett's reputation as well as suggest Garrett was a murderer. On the other hand, if they were good friends, the bond was not very strong. Maxwell broke the relationship and did not keep

Garrett's secret, ultimately bringing discredit to Garrett, anyway. Who knows Maxwell's motivation? Truthful or not, we have no way of proving the veracity of Avant's interview or Maxwell's alleged statement.

- Then there is the issue of whether the door to Maxwell's room was open or closed. Due to living in the desert southwest, most folks kept the doors closed to keep out critters such as skunks, snakes and other nefarious intruders.[6]

To suggest that people normally closed their doors is not an extensive reach but only an educated guess. To say the stories provided by Garrett and Poe were inconsistent with the truth is an overreach. Whether open or closed, either person leaving that part out of his description of events could, once again, be merely a judgment call on what was important to him.

- Entering Maxwell's house, unannounced, knowing that he might encounter a convicted killer of a sheriff and two deputies, Garrett went in without the backup of Deputies Poe and McKinney.[7]

Was this incompetence? Surely it was. However, can we conclude that Garrett and Poe lied about the incident from their description of the episode? They may have, but the only thing we can infer is that if the event happened as they describe, their judgment might have been fatal for them. To suggest that this method of seeking the outlaw is beyond rational acceptance in the law enforcement world, by two professionals no less, is another overreach. The concept makes for great debate, but is unrealistic.

Historically, law enforcement reports are rife with examples of officer misjudgments. Many officers have lost their lives because they were impatient, lacked excellent judgment skills, and they entered a building without adequate backup. In the past 40 years, I have attended many funerals of those seasoned officers who were the victims of a lapse in judgment. Both Garrett and Poe could have lied about the steps they took, but if they didn't, they were at least, lucky.

- A few moments after Garrett entered Maxwell's bedroom, deputies Poe and McKinney described a man walking in stocking feet and buttoning his pants as he approached them from the street. Both Garrett and Poe said the man was carrying a six-shooter in one hand and a butcher knife in the other. Sederwall questioned how the man could have been carrying these items and buttoning his pants at the same time.[8]

I concur. That would have been a feat for most males if not at least, cumbersome. Something akin for some folks to chewing gum and walking at the same time; challenging but not impossible. Wearing socks in this environment is undoubtedly another concern. Is it logical a person would intentionally do this? Probably not. But to anyone who understands adolescence, while seeming illogical, it is not shocking. The neurochemical reward system in the Kid's adolescent brain would likely have contributed to his faulty judgment. The thought of having fresh meat in the frying pan superseded the inconvenience of insects, burrs, and rocks he endured for the short distance. Does the comment, "What the hell were you thinking," ring a bell? Does this action strain logic? Of course, it does! He was an adolescent, and adolescents are known for risky behavior, and they are not always logical.

- Poe said he exchanged words with the stranger saying the stranger spoke to him in Spanish, "Quién es?" Poe responded in English, "trying to reassure him." Poe said this happened a several times once the stranger backed into the shadows.[9]

Sederwall suggested that since the Kid was bilingual, it was reasonable for him to respond to Poe in English, leaving us to conclude that either, a) the stranger was not Billy the Kid who approached the lawmen, or b) the incident never happened. I propose there may have been a third reason. The Kid may have recognized he was in jeopardy and chose not to respond in English.

Why did the Kid continue into Maxwell's room? Why was Poe's description of the premises in error? Why didn't Garrett or Maxwell hear this exchange through open windows? Why did Poe allow this stranger to enter the area without warning Garrett of the intrusion? And why, after all the signs the Kid received from the residents of Fort Sumner would he allow himself to be trapped, stocking-footed, in an enclosure covered by unrecognized white guys?

To accept that the Kid was infallible is irrational. The Kid had a history of mistakes and misdeeds going back to his youth. Nothing he did should surprise us. While I agree that a rational Billy would have engaged the deputies rather than pause long enough to ask questions, nothing so far refutes the possibility that Billy made some serious mistakes that cost him his life. As for Garrett and Poe lying about the incident, the *"deconstruction, analysis, and reconstruction,"* conducted by Sederwall fails to prove the incident never happened or that Garrett and Poe, *"manufactured"* their versions. His efforts only suggest questions for which no answers will be forthcoming, ever.

While I question some of Sederwall's adjudications of the previous questions, in no way am I prepared to take issue with all his findings. I have known Steve Sederwall both professionally and as a friend for over 25 years. I began my association with him when I hired him as a Special Agent in the Santa Fe Law Enforcement Division of the Bureau of Land Management in 1989. He is a consummate professional investigator, and I have known only a few who possessed his skills or imagination. Over several years Sederwall discussed with me his discoveries and discrepancies concerning Billy the Kid, many findings of which I concurred. I always thought it odd that before Sederwall's efforts, no one else considered these factors.

He recognized the discrepancies in the accounts of Garrett and Poe regarding several points. How was the Kid shot? There are questions about the number of shots; the differences in what Maxwell, Garrett, and the Kid saw in Maxwell's dark bedroom; the events after the shooting including the location of the body; the participation of Deluvina Maxwell, and the handling of the body purported to be that of the Kid. Did the person Garrett shot have a gun and a knife or just a knife? Was a drop-gun placed in the hand of the victim? What were Garrett's position and location when he fired a second shot that perforated the washstand in Maxwell's bedroom?

Sederwall was the first to engage other law enforcement officials who are experts in high stress shooting incidents. The expert analysis provided by David A. Brewer of the Federal Law Enforcement Training Center in Artesia, New Mexico, presents a professionally accepted account of physiological functions experienced by law enforcement officers during shooting incidents. In my experience, his presentation was entirely accurate. Subsequently, based on the consolidated information provided by Sederwall and Brewer's description of physiological responses during officer-involved shootings, there is undoubtedly room to consider that Garrett fabricated his explanation of the shooting event.

However, there is one possible explanation that is missing.

No one has accounted for "luck." Garrett may have been lucky the Kid didn't shoot first, and the Kid, unlucky that he didn't dodge a bullet; if the dead guy was the Kid. If luck was the only determining factor, one could understand why Garrett would lie to cover up his misjudgments. The fickle finger of fate would point squarely at Garrett, demonstrating that instead of the law enforcement professional as he wished to be recognized, he was an ignorant, self-aggrandizing fool.

Both Sheriff Garrett and Deputy Poe gave differing accounts of what happened that night in Fort Sumner. Sederwall suggested that there was an alternate universe at that moment, or they lied about what happened. Was the victim lying face down or face up? Was the victim removed and relocated to the workbench in the carpenter shop or did he remain on the floor in Maxwell's bedroom? Who entered the room first after the shooting? Why all the discrepancies about the sequencing surrounding the shooting?

Then, there are issues about the coroner's jury and the participation of the members. Nothing about the inquest seems to make sense unless one believes that Garrett and Poe both lied about the sequence of events. Sederwall is correct when he declared, ". . . there is something wrong here." Nothing was cut and dried. There is a mismatch of accounts; separately and collectively suggestive of deception.

It may be unfair to compare these cowpunchers turned lawmen with lawmen of today. These lawmen had no formal training, no law enforcement or criminal justice skills other than what they acquired by trial and error, and considering their past histories, weren't the most credible of individuals. Could it be that due to their fears, believing they did something wrong when maybe they didn't, caused them to lie about the circumstances? Murder is a strong motivator and fearing Garrett shot the wrong man would be enough to cover up the incident. Did Garrett and Poe lie independently or collectively? Probably, maybe, possibly, or all the above, Sederwall deductively concluded that there was wrongdoing on the part of the lawmen and with good reason.

Beyond doubt, there are so many inconsistencies in the accounts of that night that they cloud one's efforts to reach rational conclusions. Narratives of both Pat Garrett and John Poe differed frequently and surely suggest they didn't get their acts together to match stories, at least in the beginning. Each provided different explanations as to why they decided to search for the Kid in Fort Sumner. Neither provided an agreed-upon account on how they learned the location of the Kid. How did the Kid appear in Maxwell's room? Did he suddenly appear or did he slowly back in as he was facing Poe on the porch? Was the Kid in possession of a .41 caliber pistol, a .38 caliber pistol or no pistol at all, when he died? How many times was the Kid transferred from Maxwell's room to the carpenter's shed? Or was he moved at all? Was he lying face up or face down? Why did Poe first suggest that Garrett shot the wrong man and then change is mind?

There are doubtless inconsistencies regarding the coroner's juries. How many were there? If there was more than one coroner's jury, why? When did they occur and who participated? Allegedly, at least one account was written in English by Garrett but what of the other written in Spanish? Persistent searches of administrative records have failed to locate a recorded coroner's verdict. Was it never filed and if not, why not?

Can we believe any of the reports that the Kid's friends saw him days and weeks later after Garrett allegedly killed him? Supposedly, someone saw him in Lincoln, Seven Rivers, and Taos, New Mexico, as well as Guadalajara, Mexico; mistaken identity or intentional obfuscation? Indeed, the allegation that Garrett's daughter, Elizabeth, stated to interviewer Paul Cain in 1983, that her father did not kill the Kid, places a shroud over any conclusion to the contrary. Can we consider this as evidence or an anecdotal accounting?

Was there a coverup? One can be confident that conflicts in the story will always remain. Where is the proof, legal or otherwise that Pat Garrett killed the Kid in Fort Sumner on July 14, 1881? Only conjecture exists. Conflicting stories and no factual evidence constitute a historical crime mystery. Neither you, the reader, nor Sederwall, nor for that matter, any one of a hundred authors including me, can provide closure. Without a resurrection of William H. Bonney, alias Billy the Kid, no answers will be forthcoming. The end of his history was an unproven death.

---

[1] Garrett, Pat F. *The Authentic Life of Billy, the Kid, the Noted Desperado of the Southwest, Whose Deeds of Daring and Blood Made His Name a Terror in New Mexico, Arizona and Northern Mexico.* New Mexican printing and publishing co., 1882.

[2] Jameson, W. C. *Billy the Kid: Investigating History's Mysteries.* Twodot Publishing, 2018.

[3] Ibid. (p. 136)

[4] Ibid. (p. 136)

[5] Ibid. (p. 136)

[6] Ibid. (p. 138)

[7] Ibid. (p. 138)

[8] Ibid. (p. 139)

[9] Ibid. (p. 140)

CHAPTER 3

Abandonment and Loyalties Lost

WHEN YOU LOOK AT a tintype photographic reproduction of Billy the Kid, posing with his Winchester rifle and six-shooter, what do you see? Do you see a stalwart crusader standing with a determined look of independence, displaying the tools of his trade? Or do you see an impish-looking character with anatomical abnormalities exhibiting a look of vagueness with no spark in his eyes? What are the differences between Billy and thousands of young males who have been photographed in independent and resolute poses in uniforms of their times displaying paraphernalia indicative of their professions? We have seen them in military uniforms, cowboy garb, sports equipment, and professional displays of confidence and individuality since the advent of pictures. What makes them all similar? What makes them different?

The Kid may have technically been a crusader, but not necessarily by choice. He was a product of his environment and adolescent development. More than likely, he was fighting to survive rather than fighting for or against an ideology. Let us examine his progress from an early age up to and including his experiences in the early 1880s. What we know of his pubescent growth is somewhat limited; except we believe he had some form of structure as a child brought about mainly through the efforts of his mother. We don't know anything about the loss of his birth father, but we can surmise that the absence probably created some void in his psyche concerning the lack of a male figure in his life. However long that circumstance may have lasted or the impact of a stepfather on his development, we can only guess.

While she was alive, Billy's mother kept him emotionally grounded, and she secured his early education. We have seen evidence of both in letters he wrote to Governor Lew Wallace and others. His style of writing exhibits both an innate intellect and some quality in both the presentation and use of the English language. His grammar and word usage also present markers displaying his limitations that resulted from an interruption in the flow of his formal learning. We will examine these factors later in the chapter, but for now, let's continue with his adolescent development.

Historical accounts suggest that Billy was slight-of-frame during his youth and early teens. He lacked the strength of other boys his age. His small stature, hands, and feet made him vulnerable to men larger than him and an easy target for tormentors. He overcame these deficiencies through cunning and superior skill in the use of firearms. These advantages leveled the playing field for him and became his equalizers. Coupled with his intellect and more advanced education than that attributed to his peers, he was a superior adversary in most instances. These things together contributed to his self-confidence and determinations that served him well throughout his adolescence.

Now, let's examine some deterrent factors he experienced while growing to adulthood. Beginning with the loss of his father and the absence of a male figure in his life, the addition of a stepfather may have contributed to his more delinquent behavior when he was young. The records are not specific in this matter, but it doesn't seem that stepfather Henry Antrim was particularly useful in raising Billy or his brother after Antrim married Catherine. While they lived in Silver City, New Mexico, Antrim was an absentee stepfather.[1] This recorded absence would indicate a level of abandonment experienced by both boys. The death of his mother in 1874 represented a severe loss to Billy whether he acknowledged it or not. Considering Billy's age of approximately twelve years of age at the time of her death, the impact of not having an active father and the loss of the stability and nurturing provided by his mother, had to be severe. These events might have constituted the tripwire to begin the search for belonging and companionship. His associations with those whose lives shared commonalities led to comradery. And those relationships served to assuage the pain of loneliness.

Though Billy often demonstrated his propensity for independence, he often fell in with personalities who were rudimentarily flawed. Knowing the difference between right and wrong, he often engaged in practices accepted by members of his crowd; frowned upon by the upstanding citizens of New Mexico and Arizona. Often, he viewed his involvement in cattle rustling as a means to survive. And since his peers were doing the same thing, what did it matter? In his estimation, it wasn't as if those whose cattle he stole could not afford the losses. However, during this time frame, something changed in his world view. He became mindful of the fact that many of those he associated with were not his friends and he began to withdraw from them. Men like Jesse Evans, who were once close friends, became enemies and no longer shared common interests. Maybe he began to recognize the trail he was following was pointing in a direction he didn't wish to pursue. The onset of adulthood and his recognition of right and wrong were still not enough to overcome his engagement in risky behavior and to exercise poor judgment.

When Robert Tunstall employed the Kid as a ranch hand and Billy became acquainted with others who rode for the Tunstall brands, his elevated sense of loyalty kicked into overdrive and a sense of admiration developed within him. Whether or not Tunstall was as close to Billy as has been ascribed, Billy saw Tunstall as an essential figure and allowed himself to adapt to Tunstall's sense of humanity. Regardless of how Tunstall viewed the Kid, Billy admired Tunstall. With the death of Robert Tunstall, came one more loss and sense of abandonment that was detrimental to Billy's world view. His relationship with Tunstall was one he developed on his own and not that of a natural progression from birth. Subsequently, Billy's loss led to a craving for revenge and his need to make those who were responsible, pay with their lives. The next adult figure in his life with whom he developed a companionship was Dick Brewer, Tunstall's foreman and eventual leader of the Regulators. But he, too, would soon become a fatal casualty.

Billy was in search of leadership during this time, and he followed Brewer with abandon. Brewer's death by "Buckshot" Roberts at Glaser's Mill once again, significantly impacted Billy's sense of being. While not intentionally abandoned by Brewer, the loss did represent a form of abandonment to Billy causing an escalation in the intensity of his feelings for those who were once close to him yet taken from him by those he despised. Throughout the next few years, this was a pattern Billy would experience repeatedly. The only remedy he recognized was to make those responsible, pay for their deeds. Whether by his hand or by others, his motivation was most often, vengeance. During the Lincoln County War, the loss of so many close to Billy only served to harden his resolve to fight those opposing forces he viewed as having wronged him and those friends he lost. Maybe in this fashion, he could be fantasized as a crusader, but his real motivation was probably less than charitable.

The demise of his friends Tom O'Folliard and Charlie Bowdre at Fort Sumner and Stinking Springs had a piling-on effect, adding to his sense of loss and abandonment. Sometime along the way, he might have realized that by remaining on his chosen path, he would come to the same end as his friends. Unfortunately, this recognition probably contributed to that gaping hole of despair. Still, he somehow continued to maintain some sense of lightheartedness and hope that he could overcome the odds stacked against him.

Adding to his often-misplaced loyalties was his belief that Governor Lew Wallace was in his corner. Mistaken confidence that Wallace intended to exempt him for his crimes of livestock theft and the murder of Sheriff William Brady, Billy sent numerous letters to Governor Wallace, only to be unanswered. Billy did not understand what was happening behind the scenes with Governor Wallace, yet he continued believing he would be pardoned.

Governor Wallace issued the death warrant for Billy on April 30th, 1881. Whether the Governor ever intended on granting clemency to the Kid is a matter of speculation. When Billy killed Deputies Bell and Olinger to make his escape from the Lincoln County Jail, there was no turning back for him. Even if Wallace originally planned to live up to his agreement with Billy, the escape and double murder of the deputies changed his mind. When Wallace signed the death warrant for the Kid, it was clear he intended for Billy to hang. There could be no consideration for clemency from then on. In Billy's mind, however, Governor Wallace took his place among all the others who had abandoned him.

Suffering disappointment is a characteristic of human behavior. The cumulative effect of several disappointments would seem even more distressful for someone facing the gallows. Take, for example, Governor Wallace's promise to Billy of a trial for the murder of William Brady in Lincoln, New Mexico, where there were numerous knowledgeable jurors and witnesses. Billy found himself in Las Cruces being tried in the courtroom of Judge Warren Bristol, by all accounts a smug and authoritarian acolyte of the Santa Fe Ring. Judge Bristol had one goal in mind, and that was to carry out the wishes of the Ring and hang Billy Bonney.

Governor Wallace promised Billy his friend and personal attorney, Ira Leonard, would defend Billy against the charges. While successful in defeating the indictment for the murder of "Buckshot" Roberts, Leonard mysteriously withdrew from Billy's defense resulting in a court-ordered appointment of Albert J. Fountain as his attorney. Doubtful, however, was Fountain's success against an all Hispanic, non-English speaking jury, and there was no translation of the testimony. The trial record demonstrated that even the instructions to the jury avoided the criteria necessary to convict for premeditated murder. Judge Bristol ensured the death sentence by instructing the jury to consider as a matter of guilt that Billy, ". . . was present at the time and place of the killing and encouraged, incited, aided in, abetted, advised or commanded such killing." By these standards, Billy could have been an observer looking on from a street corner, yelling, "shoot the bastard," probably resulting in a conviction of murder in the first degree.

With only thirty days to obtain a new attorney, locate witnesses and file for an appeal, Billy needed money. His only resource was the recovery of his horse from Frank Stewart, one of Garrett's posse men, who confiscated it when Garrett arrested Billy at Stinking Springs. Attorney Edgar Caypless had been engaged on contingency by Billy to file a replevin to retrieve the horse. However, Stewart sold the horse to Winfred Scott who, in turn, gave the horse to his wife, Minnie. A contested effort ensued to repossess the mare and Billy remained without funds. His friends in Lincoln, including Susan McSween, were no help either. No one came to Billy's defense. He was on his own, and this was another bitter disappointment.

From the time Billy was incarcerated at the Lincoln County Courthouse until he escaped, he endured endless bullying and abuse by Deputy Bob Olinger. Great satisfaction and an immediate sense of euphoria occurred when he shot Olinger in the chest. He carried out his promise to kill Olinger, and this single effort provided momentary relief from all the disappointments accumulated up to this time.

Billy made his escape five days before he was to be hanged and made his way to Fort Sumner. No one believed he would be so brash as to return to the one place lawmen would obviously look for him. But in truth, it wasn't so obvious to the lawmen. No one looked for him there until word reached Garrett of Billy's presence in Fort Sumner. Despite the repeated pleas from his friends for Billy to leave Fort Sumner and head for Mexico, he refused to do so. Many believed that he intended to reason with Pat Garrett and try to explain his dilemma while others said he stayed to kill Garrett and John Chisum. I think Fort Sumner was the only real home Billy had. The nurturing and friendship of the settlement were all Billy had remaining, and he risked being captured to live for a time, free and unconstrained.

No one should be surprised that Billy engaged in this risky behavior. He had a history of rash decisions even though he was intelligent and better educated than most of his peers. Why would a young man, who had demonstrated on so many occasions his planning abilities, risk capture and death when his obvious choice for survival was to leave Fort Sumner and head for Mexico? It was because even though Billy was now nineteen years of age, he was still an adolescent. Not until the recent past have neuroscientists learned the real impact of what this means for young people today and certainly not for Billy the Kid in the 1880s.

---

[1] Nolan, Frederick W. *The West of Billy the Kid.* University of Oklahoma Press,, 1998.

CHAPTER 4

An Adolescent Life

WITH THE TINTYPE PHOTOGRAPH and his letters to Governor Lew Wallace, it's possible to assess the Kid's anatomy and his psychological condition. Ultimately, we can compare his physical and mental conditions with those of the personalities who claimed to be him in what was proscribed to be his later years.

Some authors present you with the question, "Are you going to believe me or your lying eyes?" Rather than rely on regurgitated myths, cross-eyed illustrations, and distorted historical accounting, I prefer a more methodological approach supported by forensic anthropology, medical science, and psychology. There will be some who still believe the earth is flat; our planet is the center of the universe; Elvis still lives; the Holocaust never happened; humans never landed on the moon, and Billy the Kid lived to ripe old age either as "Brushy Bill" Roberts or John Miller. Nothing presented in this book will change their minds. Despite the unwillingness of some to accept rational thought, let's begin with an examination of William Bonney, alias Billy the Kid, in terms of today's understanding of the adolescent brain and the development of judgment processes at the time of his alleged death in 1881.

Only within the last decade or so has there been a substantial study of the adolescent brain. In previous years, limited funds focused research on infant and child development, examining learning disabilities and enrichment about the end of life maladies of the aging brain. Misunderstood, underfunded, and not researched extensively, most scientists believed that child brain growth culminated somewhere between five and seven years of age. They viewed the adolescent brain, Billy the Kid's mind, to be the same as an adult's, only with fewer miles. As it turns out, that perception is incorrect.[1]

Adults view the behavior of both Billy the Kid and many of today's youth as a product of impulsiveness and hormone-driven emotions. It was easy to believe that the contrariness was because teenagers wanted to be complicated. They chose to be different and rebellious; common assumptions of Billy the Kid. The fact is that during teenage years and early adulthood, the brain has unique vulnerabilities as well as strengths. Knowing this changes our modern perspective.[2] [3]

The weighing of decisions and judgments occur behind the forehead and the frontal lobes. If we want to understand Billy's emotions, impulsivity, lack of attention, or spontaneous joy, one must look at the brain circuits and connections. While hormones do explain some of Billy's actions, hormonal chemicals can result in instability among neurotransmitters. Because of the unlimited flexibility and physiological changes to his brain during his youth, he had a capacity for extraordinary accomplishment. The downside to this flexibility was that these changes were often adversely affected by stress and radical environmental stimuli. When we examine Billy's history, we can quickly identify the stressful times and the oppositional events which represented significant markers in his development.[4]

During this time, Billy's recalcitrant behavior was not so much about risk-taking but rather about rebellion against authority. It only makes sense that a youth exercises this time of life to separate from the comfort and safety of home and parents to find independence through exploration. However, Billy had none of those from which to voluntarily separate. He was propelled into abandonment and separation not by choice but by circumstance. Unfortunately, at this time of life, his frontal cortex was underdeveloped, and he had difficulty understanding the future consequences of his actions. No different than the youth of today, he was not equipped to anticipate long-term ill-effects of his risky behavior.[5]

Billy's reasoning abilities were, more than likely, fully developed by the age of fifteen or so. He would have been just as adept at logically assessing danger as any adult. However, the reward system within Billy's brain was more intense, the same as today's youth, due to the release and effect of dopamine. Thus sensational-seeking behavior as Billy demonstrated on numerous occasions occurred at a time when neural control systems of arousal and reward were particularly sensitive. Also, his frontal lobes—the decision center—were loosely connected to other parts of the brain. Subsequently, he had a harder time assessing risks and consequences. Scientists have learned that the most significant predictor of adolescent behavior is the anticipation of reward despite the risk rather than the recognition of the risk itself. In other words, Billy focused more on what rewards he might gain from risk-taking rather than the act itself.[6]

We have learned not to underestimate peer pressure in adolescent behavior. Had his peers been more socially grounded, he would have most likely been less inclined to engage in risky and often illegal behavior. Not a hard and fast rule; more a probability. But social information, as well as emotions, factor extensively in decision-making. We have learned that the more feeling involved, the more prone a person is to take risks. There is a crucial factor here. Billy's brain areas associated with the perception of risk and reward evaluation linked closely with the region regulating behavior and emotion. The relationship means that he had outstanding cognitive abilities and learning capacity because of the discriminating synapsis of his childhood brain. He was able to gain expertise in some issues at a young age, such as the use of his firearms and his ability to shoot. But he was also vulnerable to learning the wrong lessons—associations with criminals and his propensity for livestock theft being prime examples. Again, nothing we describe of Billy's behavior is dissimilar with those behaviors of today's youth. Emotion, not reason, is what motivated many of Billy's actions.[7]

Adults can rely on the prefrontal cortex within the frontal lobes to control anger and fear. The problem is that the frontal lobes are not fully developed until the age of twenty-five or so. At the age of nineteen, Billy's brain had not fully developed. Subsequently, his reasoning capacity was severely limited. Adding to this factor is the increase of the neurochemical, cortisol. Stress, worry, anxiety, anger, and especially loneliness, associate with higher levels of cortisol. Cortisol is known to heighten emotion, anxiety, and stress.[8] No one can dispute the distress and loneliness experienced by Billy during his adolescence ranging from the loss of his mother and friends to his feelings of abandonment in his last days.[9] Considering all that Billy experienced in his life, he was remarkably well-adjusted in his dealings with others. This trait may be chalked up to resilience. A learned behavior, Billy was resilient in handling adversity. Described as a positive person, forward-thinker and planner, Billy's resilience overcame his feelings of despair.[10]

There was also rigidity in Billy's personality, and that may have been one of the reasons he stayed in Fort Sumner when he should have moved on. It was risky behavior, but his sense of reward, his sense of belonging to that community of friends, created an atmosphere of camaraderie and to some degree, contributed to his sense of invincibility. No different than that of a teenager of today driving drunk or using illicit drugs; absent recognition of potentially harmful future consequences impaired by a disconnected locus of control and an out-of-balance chemical reward system in his brain.[11]

There are other factors to consider when evaluating Billy's progress to adulthood. B. Bradford Brown [12] suggested that there are specific psychosocial tasks adolescents must accomplish in their development:

1. To stand out—to develop an identity and pursue autonomy;

Billy certainly stood out in history. He developed a well-recognized identity, and he lived by a code he created for himself. One could easily describe Billy as being autonomous.

2. To fit in—to find comfortable affiliations and gain acceptance from peers;

While his peers may not have been the best of choices, he developed relationships that were comfortable to him. Long after his alleged death, he was still admired by those who thought well of him when he was alive. Even his enemies recognized him as a worthy and dangerous opponent, universally accepted him as one of the most historic outlaws of his time.

3. To measure up—to develop competence and find ways to achieve;

Billy became an expert with firearms and was undoubtedly an accomplished rustler. He gained acceptance among his peers; those who knew him well were cautious in how they dealt with him.

4. To take hold—to make commitments to particular goals, activities, and beliefs.

Billy believed in being a gentleman around women and was never known to disparage them. He was courteous and discrete. As to his goals, Billy seemed to live from day-to-day. Long-term goals appeared to be absent except that he ultimately wanted to be treated fairly. Billy recognized his actions were often illegal, but the Kid did not escalate his routine escapades to levels of pure criminality. In other words, he avoided being a bank or stagecoach robber, and he wasn't a murderer since he didn't kill anyone who, in his mind, didn't deserve to die. However, Billy's peers, engaged in risk-taking behavior, and this was the norm. Thus, Billy's social surroundings made it more likely that he would be prone to taking risks himself.

In the end, Billy may have reasoned that the risk of remaining in Fort Sumner was worthwhile. The reward was his opportunity to set things straight with Pat Garrett and live the remainder of his life unencumbered. Had his brain been fully developed, he would have intuitively recognized that the significance of this reward was irrelevant since the risk was to be catastrophic.

----

[1] Jensen, Frances E. and Amy E. Nutt. *The Teenage Brain: A Neuroscientist's Survival Guide to Raising Adolescents and Young Adults.* HarperCollins Publishers, 2015.(p. 3)

[2] Sampson, Ovetta and Gazette The. "Brain Storm/ Can't Figure out Why Teens Act the Way They Do? Some Scientists Suggest It May Be All in Their Heads." *The Gazette*, 03/11/

2002 Mar 11 2002, p. LIFE1. ProQuest Central, https://search.proquest.com/docview/268216258?accountid=36783 https://search.proquest.com/docview/268216258?accountid=36783.

[3] Jensen, Frances E. and Amy E. Nutt. *The Teenage Brain: A Neuroscientist's Survival Guide to Raising Adolescents and Young Adults.* HarperCollins Publishers, 2015. (p. 5)

[4] Ibid.(p.4)

[5] Sandhu, Damanjit et al. "Adolescent Risk-Taking and Parental Attachment." *Indian Journal of Health and Wellbeing*, vol. 8, no. 11, 2017, pp. 1386-1392, ProQuest Central, https://search.proquest.com/docview/1986588826?accountid=36783 .

[6] Galván, Adriana. "Insights About Adolescent Behavior, Plasticity, and Policy from Neuroscience Research." *Neuron*, vol. 83, no. 2, 2014, pp. 262-265, ProQuest Central, doi:http://dx.doi.org/10.1016/j.neuron.2014.06.027.

[7] Ellis, Wendy E. et al. "The Role of Peer Group Aggression in Predicting Adolescent Dating Violence and Relationship Quality." *Journal of Youth and Adolescence*, vol. 42, no. 4, 2013, pp. 487-499, Psychology Database, doi:http://dx.doi.org/10.1007/s10964-012-9797-0.

[8] Arain, Mariam et al. "Maturation of the Adolescent Brain." *Neuropsychiatric Disease and Treatment*, vol. 9, 2013, pp. 449-461, ProQuest Central, doi:http://dx.doi.org/10.2147/NDT.S39776.

[9] Tyrka, Audrey R. et al. "Childhood Parental Loss and Adult Psychopathology: Effects of Loss Characteristics and Contextual Factors." *International Journal of Psychiatry in Medicine*, vol. 38, no. 3, 2008, pp. 329-344, ProQuest Central, https://search.proquest.com/docview/196305987?accountid=36783.

[10] Galván, Adriana. "Insights About Adolescent Behavior, Plasticity, and Policy from Neuroscience Research." *Neuron*, vol.

83, no. 2, 2014, pp. 262-265, ProQuest Central, doi:http://dx.doi.org/10.1016/j.neuron.2014.06.027.

[11] Smith, Ashley R. et al. "Peers Influence Adolescent Reward Processing, but Not Response Inhibition." *Cognitive, Affective and Behavioral Neuroscience*, vol. 18, no. 2, 2018, pp. 284-295, ProQuest Central, doi:http://dx.doi.org/10.3758/s13415-018-0569-5.

[12] Institute of Medicine (US) and National Research Council (US) Committee on the Science of Adolescence. The Science of Adolescent Risk-Taking: Workshop Report. Washington (DC): National Academies Press (US); 2011. Available from: https://www.ncbi.nlm.nih.gov/books/NBK53418/ doi: 10.17226/12961

CHAPTER 5

Anatomy as Evidence

BEYOND THE ANECDOTAL evidence presented by so many witnesses and participants in the life of Billy the Kid, there are only two types of evidence that can be attributed directly to him. These include the tintype photograph of Billy and his letters written before and during his incarceration. The first provides us with a view of his physical existence, and the second provides insight into his psychology. While the tintype photo is of poor quality and may not represent his general physical state, it does suggest some physiological problems with which he may have been born. We will discuss the relevance of his writings later, but for now, let's focus on his physical appearance.

We have all had photographs taken during times we were not at our best. These range from times when we were recuperating from a cold or the flu. The circumstances may have been the same when Billy posed for this photograph. However, there are certain features in the photo, which would not change no matter how he was feeling at the time. Those include his facial features and his shoulders.

There have been numerous facial comparisons made with other personalities in efforts to prove or disprove that Billy the

Kid lived beyond July 14, 1881. Some appeared compelling, while others were less than convincing. Had the facial features of the photograph been less distorted or faded, a facial comparison might have been more successful. However, fading, wear and tear on the photo have caused blemishes and blurring to appear. Any resemblance to another photo is probably a waste of time, and the results will nearly always be questionable.

While I'm not a physician, I have had some modicum of training in human anatomy. I have spent a significant amount of time with medical examiners during autopsies, observing outcomes of all manners of death. It is amazing what one remembers about corpses and the volume of details provided by pathologists. I also know how to research medical journals, and it's no surprise the amount of information available about human anatomy. Thus, I was curious about what appeared to be facial abnormalities along with the narrow girth and rounding of Billy's shoulders.

Anatomical growth in human beings begins in the womb and continues through adolescence. By age sixteen to eighteen, 95% of the bone structure has become rigid or ossified, and growth has ceased. By the age of twenty-five, the skeletal structure has fully developed. In particular, the pectoral saddle or shoulder saddle has fully developed, and no further growth occurs. From this point, no new changes occur in the bone structure without some external application, such as a break, some type infirmity or surgery.[1]

A prominent feature of Billy's tintype is the slope of his shoulders. In his case, the shoulders indicate a significant sloping possibly caused by small pectoral muscles and a short neck. If someone produced this photo near the age of twenty, his skeletal growth was nearly complete.

Figure 14. William H. Bonney alias Billy the Kid (Photographer Ben Wittick (1845–1903).) Public domain.

Further bone development would not have affected his shoulder girdle, and his shoulders would not have eventually become more symmetrically squared.[2] There have been suggestions that Billy had some degree of scoliosis. It is within the realm of possibility that due to poor muscle tone; scoliosis was present. However, a simple examination of the tintype is not enough to draw that conclusion.

The same is true of cranial features. While certain parts of the face continue to grow throughout life, certain features cease development and age only makes their appearance more pronounced. Common examples of this would include more elongation of the nose; ears becoming more protrusive; eyelids becoming droopier, and facial muscles appearing less rigid. However, some characteristics do not change, notably, if they are missing in the first place. A facial or cranial feature that is absent will not suddenly appear and grow over succeeding years. Positioning will also remain unchanged unless it is affected by muscle growth or atrophy.[3]

For instance, look closely at the left side of Billy's tintype photo and examine Billy's right ear. The picture presents a short, full ear morphology with small or no lobe. The outer fold or helix appears to have been snipped off. While his hat does cover some portion of his ears, he seems to have a triangular concha. His left ear is shadowed but seems similar. Decreased cartilage causes both ears to appear somewhat floppy and protrusive. His ears present to be asymmetrical as does his face in general. There may be a slight degree of facial palsy on the right side.[4]

Concerning Billy's right ear, while the image is somewhat blurred, there are distinct features. These features are critical markers for image comparisons yet so many pseudo-sleuths not educated in ear morphology, fail to recognize an ear's capacity for identification. Forensic examiners have utilized ear morphology as a means for identification of human remains since the late 19th century. Alphonse Bertillon used ear morphology as one of his eleven anthropometric measurements for his manual system of identifying individuals.[5]

From a single piece of fibrocartilage, the ear presents a complicated relief on the inside or concave side and a reasonably smooth surface on the outside or convex side. By the 38th day after birth, features of the ear become recognizable. It becomes definitive by the 56th day, and by the 70th day, one can recognize the entire shape of the ear. From then on, the development of the ear is complete and remains in the same configuration until death.[6]

While the science of ear morphology is somewhat complicated for the layperson, a simple observation of the ear without extensive measurement of the parts of the ear is often enough to make an identification. Because the human ear is unique due to its exclusive morphological structure and the organization of its various parts, defining characteristics include the following:

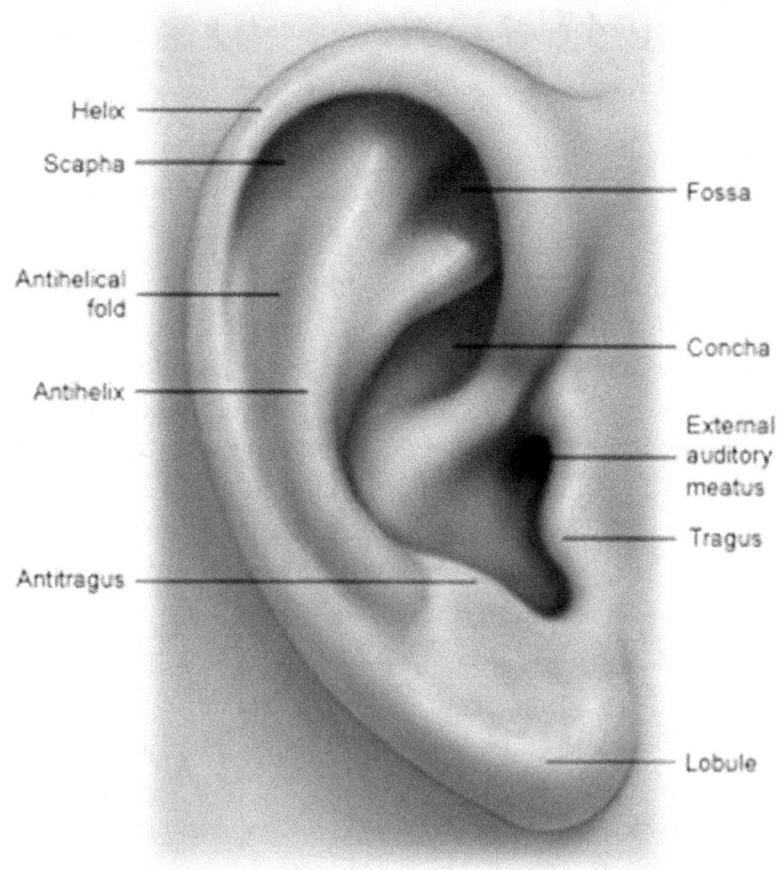

Figure 15. Ear morphology diagram of the outer ear.

1. The shape of the ear—oblique, rectangular, round or triangular;

2. The form of the helix or outer fold—concave, typically rolled, or flat;

3. The shape of the earlobe—arched, tongue, square or triangular;

4. Attachment of the earlobe—attached, free, or partially attached to the skin;

5. The thickness of the earlobe—medium, thick or thin;

6. The shape of the tragus—double knob, single knob or round;

7. Darwin's tubercle—absent, enlargement, nodosity, or projection.

A Google search of these seven elements should provide the reader with other illustrations from which to understand comparability among differing samples. Once the distinctions among these significant characteristics are understood, a layperson can draw reasonable conclusions on their own without scientific discussion.

In Billy's case, the tintype of Billy's visible right ear provides some definitive clues for comparison. Looking specifically at his earlobe, one can see that it consists of only a minor protrusion of the lobule in a square configuration. More importantly, the ear lobe is not attached to the skin of the upper neck. This feature alone will disqualify anyone claiming his identity, who has a defined earlobe attached to the surface of the high neck. Without reconstructive surgery, this configuration originated at birth, and regardless of personal explanation, will never change. That is simply a statistical validation of fact and is not scientifically disputed. If a layperson can see the configuration of the ear in multiple photographs, they can positively determine if there are significant differences. When differences are recognized, a rational conclusion exists that the photos are of different people regardless of age.

Billy also appears to have a flat midface, a small mouth, and protrusive teeth, possibly due to dental overcrowding. He exhibits a broad, prominent forehead, even though his hat covers much of it, and his eyebrows are slightly arched. Though his eyes are large, ptosis or droopy eyelids partially obscure them; an abnormality shared with prominent celebrity, Forest Whitaker.[7]

All these features presented in totality allow one to more closely examine comparative photos of others who claim the persona of Billy the Kid. What is essential to consider is that some of these features may be the result of one or more genetic disorders and may accompany other symptoms not yet identified in Billy the Kid. In the next chapter, we will consider psychiatric evidence that suggests his health and possible inherited illnesses were of significant concern to Billy.

A critical factor in discovering these features is that none of them are self-correcting. If one has no ear lobes by age twenty, they will not miraculously grow during the aging process. Ptosis of the eyelids will only become more pronounced with age, and nothing short of surgical correction will change that condition. Throughout fifty to seventy years, a small mouth remains the same. The skeletal structure does not improve with age once it is fully developed and becomes rigid. The angle of sloping shoulders will stay the same; only the muscle growth may change. Facial palsy does not correct itself nor do eyebrows change their shape by themselves. In summary, rather than trying to compare general similarities of photographs as many have done, it is more prudent to compare specific cranial, facial, and skeletal details of genetic origin that cannot be changed. If they exist on one individual and not another, then even a layperson can determine that two photos are not of the same person.

---

[1] Land, C. and E. Schoenau. "Fetal and Postnatal Bone Development: Reviewing the Role of Mechanical Stimuli and Nutrition." *Best Pract Res Clin Endocrinol Metab*, vol. 22, no. 1, 2008, pp. 107-118, doi:10.1016/j.beem.2007.09.005.

[2] Pu, Qin et al. "Development of the Shoulder Girdle Musculature." vol. 245, no. 3, 2016, pp. 342-350, doi:10.1002/dvdy.24378.

[3] Akbari, Mohammad Reza et al. "Facial Asymmetry in Ocular Torticollis." *Journal of current ophthalmology*, vol. 27, no. 1-2, 2015, pp. 4-11, PubMed, doi:10.1016/j.joco.2015.10.005.

[4] Traboulsi, Elias I. "Congenital Abnormalities of Cranial Nerve Development: Overview, Molecular Mechanisms, and Further Evidence of Heterogeneity and Complexity of Syndromes with Congenital Limitation of Eye Movements." *Transactions of the American Ophthalmological Society*, vol. 102, 2004, pp. 373-389, PubMed, https://www.ncbi.nlm.nih.gov/pubmed/15747768 https://www.ncbi.nlm.nih.gov/pmc/articles/PMC1280110/.

[5] Kaushal, Nitin and Purnima Kaushal. "Human Earprints: A Review." *Journal of Biometrics and Biostatistics*, vol. 2, 2011.

[6] Verma, Pradhuman et al. "Morphological Variations and Biometrics of Ear: An Aid to Personal Identification." *Journal of clinical and diagnostic research : JCDR*, vol. 10, no. 5, 2016, pp. ZC138-ZC142, PubMed, doi:10.7860/JCDR/2016/18265.7876.

[7] Pavone, P. et al. "Ptosis in Childhood: A Clinical Sign of Several Disorders: Case Series Reports and Literature Review." *Medicine*,

vol. 97, no. 36, 2018, pp. e12124-e12124, PubMed, doi:10.1097/MD.0000000000012124.

CHAPTER 6

Content Analysis of Verbal Behavior

I DESCRIBED THE PSYCHIATRIC science used for the examination of written documents in Appendix VI, including the techniques and their origins so readers could review for themselves and understand that analysis of Billy's letters is based on long-established and extensively validated scientific methodology and not some voodoo science. The Appendix Scales I–V only demonstrate the statistical outcomes and the resulting analyses. Using this methodology, we look at the letters Billy wrote during the last established years of his life and attempt to determine what may have been the impact of his environment and experiences during his adolescence.

So many texts and articles described Billy as an impetuous and unbalanced youth. Many called him a psychotic killer while others referred to him as a crusader, I think he was merely trying to survive the hazardous situations in which he so often found himself. I had no preconception of his mental state except to understand that adolescent development was not on the radar during the late 1800s and only because of the recent research in neurobiology has there been any attempt to appreciate juvenile evolution. We have only learned about what makes our kids tick in the last ten years. So, conducting psychiatric content analysis promised to be very enlightening. I was not disappointed.

Under normal circumstances, psychiatric or psychological diagnosis requires numerous sessions with mental health clinicians. These sessions did not happen during Billy's lifetime, and of course, after his demise, a psychological autopsy can only examine his actions during his life. While this might provide a profile of Billy's persona, it would be difficult to determine his mental health status. In the 1960s, Louis A. Gottschalk and Goldine Gleser developed a process to assess the psychiatric states of an individual.[1] They used content analysis to measure verbal responses, in short, open-ended statements. They understood that spoken language not only conveys information a speaker intended to communicate; it also reveals information about a speaker he or she did not expect to deliver. Ultimately, Gottschalk and Gleser identified thirty-three standardized scales and subscales used to examine verbal responses. This method assesses what people say or write and how strongly they feel about their subject matter. They called the technique, *Content Analysis of Verbal Behavior*, and for over fifty years, the method has not only been well established and validated, the process is currently in use among multiple disciplines and fields such as medicine, surgery, psychiatry, nursing, psychoanalysis, psychology, sociology, history, marketing, advertising, business management, and even in criminal investigations.[2] Notably, this method was used to effectively evaluate the psychiatric conditions of Napoleon Bonaparte[3] and Mahatma Gandhi.[4]

While this information might be more in-depth than the reader probably needs, I wanted to include it so that there is an understanding that procedures used in the analysis of Billy's writings have no basis in conjecture or some unproven processes. These methods work, and I'm surprised researchers haven't more extensively utilized them before now. Unfortunately, there were only a few samples of Billy's writing, and these were limited to letters written to Governor Lew Wallace and friends. Billy wasn't known to have engaged in extensive written communications. Therefore, I could only perform a limited analysis. Even so, the results were significant in that they provided a snapshot of Billy's mental health during the last couple of years before his alleged demise.

Copies of the seven letters and notes Billy wrote to Governor Wallace were obtained from the Lew Wallace Collection of the Indiana Historical Society and converted to text format.

W. H. Bonney Letter to Friend Wilson, March 20, 1879[5]

San Patricio

Thursday. 20th. 1879

Friend Wilson.

Please tell you know who that I do not know what to do, now as those Prisoners have escaped. To Send word by bearer. a note through You it may be that he has made different arrangements if not and he still wants it the same to Send (William Hudgins) as Deputy, to the Junction tomorrow at three o'clock with some men you know to be all right. Send a note telling me what to do

W H Bonney

P.S. do not Send Soldiers

Letter Fragment by Billie, 1879[6]

On the Pecos, all that I can remember are the so-called Dolan outfit, but they are all up here now and on the Rio Grande. This man Cris Molen I believe his name is, he drove a herd of 80 head one year ago
Last December in company with Frank Wheeler Frank Baker deceased, Jesse Evans (Jesse Evans) George Davis alias Tom Jones, Tom Hill his name in Texas being Tom Chelson also deceased. They drove the cattle to the Indian Reservation and sold them to John Riley and JJ Dolan, and the cattle were turned in for Beef for the Indians the Beckwith family made their boasts that they came to Seven Rivers a little over four years ago with one Milk Cow borrowed from John Chisum they had when I was there Year ago one thousand six hundred head of the male members of cattle The family are (is) Henry Beckwith and John Beckwith Robert Beckwith was killed the time McQueen's house was burned. Charles Robert Olinger and Wallace Olinger are of the same gang. Their cattle ranch is situated at Rock Corral twelve miles below Seven Rivers on the Pecos. Paxton and Pierce are still below them forty miles from Seven Rivers there are four of them Paxton: Pierce: Jim Raymen and Breck Powel. They had

when I seen them last about one thousand head of cattle: at Rocky Arroya there is another Ranch belonging to Smith who operated on the Penaco last year with the Jesse Evans gang. Those and the places I mentioned are all I know of this man Cris Moten at the time they stole those cattle was in the employ of J. J. Dolan an Co I afterwards Seen Some of the cattle at the Rinconada Bonita on the reservation those were the men we were in search of when we went to the Agency. the Beckwith family were attending to their own business when this War Started, but G.W. Peppin told them that this was John Chisums war and so they took a hand thinking they would loose their cattle in case that he Chisum won the fight this is all the information I can give you on this point

Yours Respectfully Billie

W.H. Bonney Letter to Lew Wallace, March 20, 1879[7]

San Patricio
Lincoln County(Bonney
Thursday 20th, 1879
General Lew. Wallace:
Sir, I will keep the appointment I made but be Sure and

have men come that You can depend on I am not afraid to die like a man fighting, but I would not like to be killed like a dog unarmed. tell Kimbal to let his men be placed around the house. and for him to come in alone; and he can arrest us. all I am afraid of is that in the Fort we might be poisioned or killed through a Window at night. but you can arrange that all right. tell the Commanding Officer to watch (Lt. Goodwin) he would not hesitate to do anything there will be danger on the road of Somebody waylaying us to kill us on the road to the Fort.

You will never catch those fellows on the road. Watch Fritzes, Captain Bacas ranch and the Brewery they will either go to Seven Rivers or to Picarillo Montians they will stay around close until the scouting parties come in. give a Spy a pair of glasses and let him get on the mountain back of Fritzes and watch and if they are there, there will be provisions carried to them. it is not my place to advise you, but I am anxious to have them caught, and perhaps know how men hide from Soldiers better than you. please excuse me for having so much to Say and I still remain Yours Truly

W H. Bonney

P.S.

I have changed my mind Send Kimbal to Gutieres just

below San Patricio one mile because Sanger and Ballard are or were great friends of Caniels Ballard told me [crossed out text: today] yesterday to leave for you were doing everything to catch me. it was a blind to get me to leave tell Kimbal not to come before 8 oclock for I may not be there before.

William Bonney Letter to Lew Wallace, December 12, 1880[8]

Fort Sumner
Dec 12th, 1880
Gov. Lew Wallace
Dear Sir
I noticed in the Las Vegas Gazette a piece which stated that, Billy the Kid, the name of which I am known in the Country was the Captain of a Band of Outlaws who hold Forth at the Portales. There is no such organization in Existence. So, the Gentleman must have Drawn very heavily on his Imagination. My bussinness at the White Oaks the time I was waylaid, and my horse Killed was to see Judge Leonard who has my case in hand. He had written to me to come up. That he thought he could get

below San Patricio one mile because Sanger and Ballard are or were great friends of Caniels Ballard told me [crossed out text: today] yesterday to leave for you were doing everything to catch me. it was a blind to get me to leave tell Kimbal not to come before 8 oclock for I may not be there before. Everything Straighend up. I did not find him at the Oaks & Should have gone to Lincoln if I had met with no accident. After mine and Billie Wilsons horses were killed, we both made our way to a Station forty miles from the Oaks kept by Mr. Greathouse. When I got up next morning the house was Surrounded by an outfit led by one Carlyle. Who came into the house and demanded a Surrender. I asked for their Papers and they had none. So, I Concluded it amounted to nothing more than a mob and told Carlyle that he would have to Stay in the house and lead the way out that night. Soon after a note was brought in Stating that if Carlyle did not come out inside of five minutes, they would kill the Station Keeper (Greathouse) who had left the house and was with them. In a Short time, a shot was fired on the outside and Carlyle thinking Greathouse was Killed jumped through the window breaking the Sash as he went and was killed by his own Party, they thinking it was me trying to make my Escape. The party then withdrew. They returned the next day and burned an old man named Spencer's house and Greathouses also I made my way to this Place afoot and During my absence Deputy Sheriff Garrett Acting under Chisums orders went to the Portalio and found Nothing. On his way back he went by Mr. Yerbys ranch and took a pair of mules of mine which I had left with Mr Bowdre who is in charge of Mr Yerbys cattle. He [Garrett] *claimed that they were stolen and Even if they were not, he had a right to Confiscate any outlaw's property. I have been at Sumner Since I left Lincoln making my living Gambling the mules were bought by me the truth of which I can prove by the best citizens around Sumner. J.S. Chisum is the man who got me into Trouble and was benefited Thousands by it and is now doing all he can against me. There is no Doubt but what there is a great deal of Stealing going on in the Territory and a great deal of the Property is taken across the Plains as it is a good outlet but so far as my being at the head of a Band there is nothing of it in several Instances I have recovered Stolen Property where there was no chance to get an Officer to do it. One Instance for Hugo Zuber Post office Puerto De Luna. Another for Pablo Analla Same Place. If some impartial Party were to investigate this matter, they would find it far Different from the impression put out by Chisum and his Tools.*

Yours Respect,
William Bonney

W. H. Bonney Note to Lew Wallace, January 1, 1881[9]

Santa Fe
Jan." 1st 1881
Gov. " Lew Wallace
Dear Sir
I would like to See you for a few moments if you can spare time
Yours Respect. "
W. H. Bonney

Wm. H. Bonney Letter to Lew Wallace, March 4, 1881[10]

Santa Fe, In Jail
March 4th, 1881
Gov. Lew Wallace
Dear Sir
I wrote you a little note the day before yesterday but have received no answer. I Expect you have forgotten what you promised me, this month two Years ago. but I have not, and

I think You had ought to have come and seen me as I requested you to. I have done Everything that I promised you I would, and you have done nothing that you promised me.

I think when you think the matter over, you will come down and See me, and I can then Explain Everything to you. Judge Leonard Passed through here on his way East in January and promised to come and see me on his way back but he did not fulfill his Promise. it looks to me like I am getting left in the Cold. I am not treated right by Sherman. he lets Every Stranger that comes to See me through Curiosity in to See me but will not let a single one of my friends in, not Even an Attorney.

I guess they mean to Send me up without giving me any show. but they will have a nice time doing it I am not intirely without friends

I shall Expect to see you Sometime today
Patiently Waiting
I am Very Truly Yours Respect
Wm. H. Bonney

W. Bonney Note to Lew Wallace, March 27, 1881[11]

Santa Fe New Mexico

March 27"/81

Gov" Lew Wallace

Dear Sir

for the last time I ask, Will you Keep your promise. I start below tomorrow Send answer by bearer

Yours Respt

W Bonney

The Analysis

It is important to note that mentally ill individuals often behave in ways that are indistinguishable from people who are mentally well. And conversely, people who enjoy good mental health can express their fear, anger, and sadness appropriately. The assessment of emotions from verbal samples may reveal an individual's reactions to distressing current events. What distinguishes mental health from mental disorders is not merely the intensity of emotional responses, but also the timeliness and appropriateness of these emotions as well as the defenses and coping mechanisms the person has available. These are matters about which the analyst must make significant judgments.

These evaluations from verbal samples can produce signs of minor and major mental disorders as well as signs of early cognitive impairment and cerebral organic malfunctioning. Trait-like features derived from five-minute oral samples are not so convincing as the averages of several five-minute (or longer) spoken samples taken over periods of days, weeks, or months. In Billy's case, several letters written over several months lend credibility and provide a broader view of his mental and physical ailments.

Single five-minute verbal samples tend to be indicative of state-like (relatively transient) psychobiological dimensions, such as the emotions of anxiety towards himself and others. However, content analysis scores of what we call social alienation-personal disorganization (precursor to schizophrenia), depression, and cognitive impairment tend to show less variation over time than the content analysis scores of anxiety or hostility, unless the subject is taking some psychoactive medication, which generally may be capable of reducing feedback derived from the content analysis. Drugs of this type might include opium, marijuana, peyote, and alcohol, none of which show prominence in Billy's history.

In the current analysis, I examined seven samples. However, the short letter samples from Billy to Lew Wallace on January 1st, 1881 and March 27, 1881, were incorporated with the letter dated March 4th, 1881. Since the process cannot reliably perform content analysis on samples of less than 80 words, I combined both samples (73 words in total) to a lengthier letter. As it turns out, neither addition had any impact on the analysis of the March 4th, message. There were also several spelling, grammatical and punctuation errors in these samples as a result of Billy's efforts and in some cases, errors in transcription due to poor quality of the document. I corrected these errors only when necessary, to conform to the examination requirements.

Concerning his letter to Friend Wilson, Billy appears to be stable and exhibits no symptoms of poor health. There is an indication that he experienced some level of anxiety during this period since there was evidence of a mildly elevated shame anxiety. And to a degree, he was experiencing some depression and self-accusation. In total, however, both his anxiety and depression were not abnormal. I would expect that his shame and self-accusation reflect hidden emotions resulting from his participation in killing several individuals and his criminal escapades. The results suggest that Billy had a conscience and he was at least, somewhat bothered by his past deeds.

Mostly, he exhibited normal behavior. He showed no signs of hostility, towards himself or others, nor was there resentment towards his circumstances as he was somewhat ambivalent. He presented no sign of social alienation-personal disorganization, which if there were signs, might indicate the onset of schizophrenia. He did not have schizophrenia, nor was he cognitively impaired. At this time, he demonstrated common goals consistent with adolescence and a quest for quality of life. Finally, there seemed to be no evidence that Billy had any mental disorders when he wrote to Friend Wilson.

The dynamics began to change somewhat in Billy's letter fragment in 1879. While his total anxiety appeared normal, he was experiencing underlying feelings regarding death and guilt. Examining this timeframe of Billy's life, one might expect that several occurrences were contributing to these feelings. These included the murder of John Tunstall, the shootout at Blazer's Mill, the killing of Sheriff William Brady, and more. Still, even considering the impact of his pre-adolescent development, he appeared to be an average functioning youth.

The most significant change exhibited in this sample, however, was how he viewed his health. Billy was preoccupied with sickness, either his own or someone else's. This preoccupation could be the result of his thinking about his mother and her struggle with tuberculosis, or he may have been experiencing some infirmity himself. At the same time, how he felt about others began to decline. While this may have been the result of a temporary or transient situation, it is the first inclination that Billy was having trouble with cordial or warm relationships. During this time, he was inclined to be pessimistic, depressed, and he struggled with some social phobia. Or, it could be that when he wrote this letter, he didn't feel well due to acute illness and did not feel like being around anyone at that moment.

Despite how Billy felt about others, achievement motivated him. Conversely, he was often frustrated at his failures. A common analogy would be ". . . the harder I work, the 'behinder' I get." Still, Billy's attention to his quality of life remained healthy, and he showed no evidence of a mental disorder.

By the time Billy wrote his letter to Lew Wallace on March 20th, 1879, we have a more explicit picture of what Billy was experiencing. He was mildly depressed, and he was having considerable trouble sleeping. Extreme focus on physical symptoms—such as pain or fatigue—characterizes anatomical concerns that caused significant emotional distress and problems functioning. Billy may or may not have had a diagnosed medical condition associated with these symptoms, but the reaction was not normal. This reaction suggests that Billy was preoccupied with his sickness, not the illness resulting in the death of his mother. During this timeframe, Billy was experiencing a severe illness. The infirmity may link to a congenital disorder described earlier, or he experienced an illness such as pneumonia, pleurisy, a severe cold or the flu. At any rate, it stands to reason that his disease adversely affected how he felt about others.

At the time of this letter, Billy experienced severe "hidden" depression. Billy may have developed an adjustment disorder mixed with anxiety and depression. However, without a clinical perspective and a physical examination, Billy's mental health is only reflective of the content analysis of his verbal behavior.

By the time Billy wrote his letter to Governor Wallace on December 12th, 1880, Billy's circumstances changed for the worse. He was there at the Greathouse Ranch when they killed James Carlyle, and he was aware that Pat Garrett was on his trail. Billy recovered somewhat from his illness, but even so, he was still preoccupied with it. Billy experienced a lessening of his physical pain but not his mental pain. He retreated from warm feelings about others and became further depressed and pessimistic; now exhibiting some level of social phobia.

Considering that others were trying to capture and possibly kill him, there wasn't much room in his heart during that time for warm and fuzzy feelings. Even so, he displayed outwardly a relatively healthy outlook on his quality of life, though inwardly not so much. The diagnostic outcomes remain suggestive that he was still depressed with some adjustment disorder but may have developed a personality disorder as well.

So, what is the difference between an adjustment disorder and a personality disorder? An adjustment disorder is a group of symptoms, such as stress, feeling sad or hopeless, and physical symptoms that can occur after you go through a stressful life event. Billy had more than a few. The symptoms occur because one is having a hard time coping. The reaction is stronger than what might be expected for that type of event. A personality disorder is a type of mental disorder in which one has a rigid and unhealthy pattern of thinking, functioning, and behaving. A person with a personality disorder has trouble perceiving and relating to situations and people. By the time he wrote this letter, his unhealthy thinking pattern was more apparent.

Billy wrote the last three messages to Lew Wallace after Garrett jailed him in Santa Fe and he awaited transport to his trial in Las Cruces, New Mexico. The analysis determined that Billy was not necessarily experiencing high anxiety, but separation from others certainly bothered him. His concern was understandable since he was, in effect, "separated" from his friends and the outside world. Still, the Kid did not appear to be hostile towards anyone other than himself. There were signals that he was experiencing a minor, emotional crisis during this stressful time, being reactive to self-criticism and depression. One might think Billy was angry about his circumstances, prone to display belligerence given the opportunity. However, he appeared ambivalent and demonstrated neither hostility toward his fate or events he couldn't control. His ego was stable, and he still displayed no indication of cognitive impairment.

By the time he wrote the letter to Lew Wallace on March 4th, 1881, Billy's health was once again of concern to him, possibly the result of another common cold or something more extreme, though no one can say with certainty. Remember that he had just experienced a rather arduous journey stemming from his dead of winter arrest and transport from Stinking Springs. His involuntary stay at the Santa Fe County Jail lacked comfort and probably contributed to poor health during this time.

Regardless, he still exhibited a possible adjustment disorder with depression or even a personality disorder. Considering all that Billy had experienced by the time he wrote the last letter to Lew Wallace, the development of some mental ailment was not unexpected.

Each letter analyzed independently allows us to view events as they happened to Billy and recognize how these events affected Billy both psychologically and physiologically. While his writing only represents a segmented snapshot of episodes in his life, we can examine them collectively and reach some reasonable conclusions about the totality of his state of mind during the years 1879 through 1881. Did we see a lack of vigor in his approach to life? Was he in declining health? How significant were his depressive states, and were they reflective of his overall well-being?

There appears to be at least a suggestion that Billy was suffering from some mental disorders by the time he was incarcerated in Santa Fe January through March of 1881. These disorders appeared progressive since the beginning analyses did not detect evidence of such. There were indications that he lamented about his incarceration, and he exhibited feelings of shame, guilt, and occasionally worried about his death. Still, these states of mind did not create uncontrollable anxiety. Maybe they were transient or short-lived feelings, but not all attributes were collectively consistent throughout the analyses.

Billy demonstrated throughout these years that he was not intellectually deficient, and he appeared to have a relatively healthy outlook on life most of the time. Considering experiences throughout his life, his survival was quite spectacular. Other than the impact of his adolescence and brain development that led to some poor life choices, Billy remained rather well-balanced, except, of course, for the occasional killing. Since he provided no written samples for examination from the time of his escape from Lincoln County Jail to the night of his alleged death in July 1881, we can't assess any psychological changes he may have experienced during that time. A forensic clinician may be able to conduct Billy's psychological autopsy, but there is no validated empirical data to accompany the assessment.

Billy exhibited bouts of depression relating to self-accusation; showing the same signs an adolescent of today might upon being caught in a compromising position. Psychologists often view rare similar traits as having resulted from having a bad day. However, it doesn't appear that Billy was as healthy as people thought. Considering his diminutive state and the environment in which he lived, pursued by lawmen and outlaws alike, his sleep patterns couldn't have been optimal either. Limited sleep and the propensity to contract minor infirmities undoubtedly aggravated his feelings of pain and discomfort.

Billy's depression occurred nearly a year after the Battle of Lincoln, New Mexico when he received a bullet wound in the upper thigh. His discomfort could have been a carry-over from the wound he received the previous year, but this is improbable because there is no suggestion of any infection or exacerbation of the injury. More than likely, Billy had contracted some illness that resulted in fever and muscle pain. Though the analysis supported the illness theory, we do not know for sure how long this illness lasted, but by December 1880, he seemed to have bounced back because both his sleeping habits and depressive states showed signs of improvement.

Billy did not seem to experience any disturbances in his coherence or logic, and while he might not have had warm feelings about his fellow man, his demonstrations of friendship and camaraderie appeared to be honorable. Even his attitudes toward some of his enemies were less than antagonistic, and he displayed no symptoms of withdrawal or avoidance. There were never any signs of a schizophrenic syndrome in this young man, and he showed continuous optimism during the period covered by these letters; he portrayed a sense of positive belief in his survival and welfare. Even during the direst of circumstances, Billy seemed to embrace his quality of life. Each of his letters substantiated this theme.

So, by using psychiatric content analysis, we can reach a substantial understanding of Billy's life throughout the years 1879 through 1881 by evaluating each of his letters during that time. We also understand more broadly how Billy experienced growth in general. When one combines the content analysis results with a historical perspective, it's easier to see that, in many ways, Billy was an average adolescent experiencing many of the same issues as those adolescents of today, except he had a gun and didn't hesitate to use it. Billy may have been an outlaw, and some would believe a scourge of Lincoln County, but I believe there is little doubt Billy was remarkable in his strength of character. And he was indeed superior in his ability to overcome social barriers, all while maintaining reasonably stable mental health. The correct and verifiable psychiatric content analysis scores strongly support that conclusion.

On the other hand, being a product of his environment and socioeconomic status do not forgive William H. Bonney for all the poor choices he made. His mother taught him from early on, the difference between right and wrong, and he frequently chose "wrong." He was a killer, and except those moments he was acting in self-defense, nothing presented here can provide him with any excuse for murder. He killed Deputies James W. Bell and Bob Olinger, one maybe out of necessity but the other, for revenge. And his shooting of Joe Grant probably met the threshold of premeditation. No matter how one spins the story, Billy was destined sooner or later for the gallows.

Content analysis also provided insight into other matters, mainly his use of specific vernacular. A study of his language delivered no significant evidence that there was hidden intent or deception in his letters. Since the letters were not open-ended statements in answer to specific questions, there was no expectation of finding either. There were however, two somewhat peculiar phrases which beg closer scrutiny. One referenced being "killed like a dog," concerning being able to defend himself. Reading "The Saga of Billy the Kid," by Walter Noble Burns, one would note that he referenced that phrase no less than five times throughout his book and maybe more. It is also a phrase that will play prominently in a future evaluation of another personality who claimed to be Billy the Kid, Oliver P. "Brushy Bill" Roberts.

Another phrase referred to Sheriff Pat Garrett confiscating his mules as stolen property from a ranch owned by Thomas Yerby, ". . . on his way back he [Garrett] went by Mr. Yerby's ranch and took a pair of mules of mine which I had left with Mr. Bowdre who is in charge of Mr. Yerby's cattle. He [Garrett]) claimed that they were stolen and even if they were not, he had a right to confiscate any outlaw's property." Billy left the mules with Charlie Bowdre who was working for Yerby. They were probably stolen since Billy owned very little that he didn't take unlawfully in the first place. Even so, Billy believed in the adage, "possession is nine-tenths of the law."

However, Garrett allegedly commented that he had a legal right to confiscate outlaw property. Garrett's philosophy was as incorrect then as it is now. Without some statutory adjudication, Garrett's removing the mules without a court order constituted an act of theft. The fact that he was beyond his jurisdiction as Sheriff of Lincoln County compounded the crime. The Yerby ranch was in San Miguel County where Garrett had no authority; if it happened at all as there was no supporting record to validate Billy's claim. The issue raised by Billy was an underlying theme later when Garrett supposedly shot him. Neither Stinking Springs nor Fort Sumner were in Lincoln County either. Both the arrest of Billy at Stinking Springs and his alleged killing at Fort Sumner should have had severe legal consequences for Garrett if he had not already stacked the deck against Billy.

And finally, a comparison of all the letters and notes Billy wrote to Lew Wallace, Squire Wilson, and his letter fragment demonstrated that in every communication except one, his signature was a derivation of William H. Bonney (e.g. W.H. Bonney, William Bonney, Wm. H. Bonney or W. Bonney). Also, within the letter to Wallace dated December 12, 1880, the Kid referenced himself, "I noticed in the Las Vegas Gazette a piece which stated that, Billy the Kid, the name of which I am known in the Country was the Captain of a Band of Outlaws who hold Forth at the Portales." For the past 138 years, in references made of the Kid, he was referred to as "Billy." In his letter fragment written 1879, he signed his name, "Billie," the only time he spelled his name with "ie" instead of "y." No one ever explained the significance of this change of spelling. Some historians believe that this note was not written by the Kid but by a woman. Use of the letters "ie" suggest a feminine approach to the spelling of his name since the letter "y" is more often the masculine version. Probably never to be proved, the question will remain unanswered. Though a minor detail, it makes for a stimulating conversation.

William H. Bonney was the most famous outlaw of not only the Old West but current times as well. In almost all languages, regardless of location in the world, people recognize the name "Billy the Kid." They may not know or understand his history, but he was and still is an international celebrity. Psycholinguistic analysis of Billy's actual language in his letters and notes to Governor Lew Wallace and friends delivers a trove of undisclosed information. Not everything written about the Kid was correct. The public only saw the Kid as an enigma. As is often the case with historical figures, storytellers embellish the facts to create the legend. In this book, I resurrect in thought not a folk hero, but the authentic William H. Bonney, alias Billy the Kid, and unmask an impostor who claimed to be him.

[1] Gottschalk, L.A. and F. Lolas. "The Gottschalk-Gleser Content Analysis Method of Measureing the Magnitude of Psychological Diminsions: Its Application in Transcultural Research." *Transcultural Psychiatric Research Review*, vol. 26, no. 2, 1989, pp. 83-777.

[2] Tunnell, Dale L. "Computerized Psychiatric Content Analysis and Diagnosis in an Investigative Environment." *Computerized Content Analysis of Speech and Verbal Texts and Its Many Applications*, edited by L.A. Gottschalk and Robert J. Bechtel, Nova Science Publishers, Inc., 2008.

[3] Gottschalk, Louis A. et al. "Computerized Content Analysis of Some Adolescent Writings of Napoleon Bonaparte: A Test of the Validity of the Method." *The Journal of Nervous and Mental Disease*, vol. 190, no. 8, 2002.

[4] Gottschalk, Louis A. and Robert J. Bechtel. "Computerized Content Analysis of Writings of Mahatma Gandhi." *The Journal of Nervous and Mental Disease* vol. 193, no. 3, 2005.

[5] Bonney, William H. "Letter to Friend Wilson." edited by Squire Wilson, Making arrangements for meeting. edition, Indiana Historical Society, 3/20/1879 1879.

[6] ---. "Letter Fragment." edited by Unknown, Description of criminal activities in Lincoln County edition, Indiana Historical Society, unknown/1879 1879.

[7] ---. "Handwritten Letter to Lew Wallace." edited by Lew Wallace, Making arrangements with Wallace for meeting. edition, Indiana Historical Society, 3/20/1879 1879.

[8] ---. "Handwritten Letter to Lew Wallace." edited by Lew Wallace, Explanation of his involvement in the Death of Jim Carlyle and other troubles. edition, Indiana Historical Society, 1880.

[9] ---. "Handwritten Note to Lew Wallace." edited by Lew Wallace, Asked Wallace to keep his promise. edition, Indiana Historical Society, 3/27/1881 1881.

10 ---. "Handwritten Letter to Lew Wallace." edited by Lew Wallace, Asking Wallace to keep promise of pardon for BTK edition, Indiana Historical Society, 3/4/1881 1881.

11 ---. "Handwritten Note to Lew Wallace." edited by Lew Wallace, Asked Wallace to keep his promise. edition, Indiana Historical Society, 3/27/1881 1881.

PART II:

UNMASKING THE IMPOSTER

CHAPTER 7

Exhumation of John Miller

WHILE WORKING AS A Special Investigator for the Professional Standards Bureau of the Arizona Department of Corrections in 2003, I had numerous conversations with an old friend and compatriot who lived in Capitan, New Mexico. Sheriff Tom Sullivan and my friend, Reserve Deputy Sheriff, Steve Sederwall of the Lincoln County Sheriff's Department were engaged in an investigation into the deaths of Deputies James Bell and Bob Olinger. Both men were killed by Billy the Kid during his escape from the Lincoln County Courthouse in Lincoln, New Mexico on April 21, 1881.

Sullivan and Sederwall were intent on setting the record straight by determining the facts of the Bell and Olinger murders. Their anticipated outcome was to present facts determined by modern-day crime scene forensics, to clear up inconsistencies presented in historical context and to place headstones on the unmarked graves of the murdered deputies. I believed they had honorable intentions. Simple, right? Not so much. No one predicted the intensity and scrutiny their investigation would eventually engender.

During their initial investigation, they discovered scientifically supported details that conflicted with historical accounts about Billy the Kid. They questioned the circumstances by which history presented about the Kid's escape from the Lincoln County Courthouse as well as his alleged death at the Pete Maxwell residence in Fort Sumner, New Mexico, on July 14, 1881. Many Billy the Kid authors based their opinions and presentations on information often exaggerated and unfounded, gleaned from anecdotal stories and fabrications. Consequently, it was often difficult to sort fact from fiction, and frequently, fabrication won out. Both Sullivan and Sederwall had years of experience as criminal investigators, and they felt that if these incidents could be looked at from a criminal investigator's point of view, backed up by proven scientific methods, they might be able to sort out what happened during those events.

While Sullivan and Sederwall were proceeding with their investigation, I was conducting internal affairs type investigations for the Arizona Department of Corrections and at the same time, pursuing my doctorate in psychology, specifically in psycholinguistics and voice analysis. I was lucky enough during my employment with the department to attend some training, which provided me with specialized skills in content analysis of written documents.

Content Analysis was one of the primary skills I had perfected at the time of my conversations with Sederwall. While he didn't particularly understand them, Sederwall was aware that with the written documents he had amassed, my skills might be invaluable to overall efforts. He asked if I was interested in becoming involved, and frankly, I was quite intrigued. I expressed my desire to become part of their efforts but was somewhat reticent because I was employed full-time and didn't have enough time on my own to pursue his investigation. I suggested that Sheriff Sullivan submit a request for assistance to my director at the Arizona Department of Corrections. Sheriff Sullivan corresponded with my department, and his letter in 2003 resulted in a self-propelled, roller coaster ride that lasted for over a decade.

I provided several updates to my administrator outlining my activities throughout 2003. One report summed up my feelings and those of Sullivan and Sederwall. I wrote: "The New Mexico Governor, Bill Richardson, has recently decided to recognize this investigation officially and has pledged financial support through the New Mexico Bureau of Tourism. He has stated that the impact on recorded history as well as the potential for increased tourism as a result of the investigation, is significant enough to warrant the involvement of his office. I have initially reviewed several supporting documents relating to the death and burial of John Miller in the Pioneer Home Cemetery in Prescott, Arizona. The existence of documents in Phoenix, Prescott, and Tucson, which pertain to this case, and the potential line to John Miller, formerly a resident of Buckeye, Arizona, and buried in Prescott in 1937, make Arizona's connection to this potentially, history-altering investigation, significant."[1]

These same sentiments were shared up the chain from the Director of the Department of Corrections to the Office of Governor, as my participation in the investigation was not only approved but encouraged. The guidance I received from the Department was simple; assist with the New Mexico investigation but continue to resolve cases assigned me as part of my job with the Administrative Investigations Unit. The effort was interruptive since we only had nine members in the unit, and our department had over 11,000 employees. In any state correctional organization, employment investigations of corruption, violations of department rules and regulations, drinking and driving arrests, family member assaults, correctional officers compromised by inmates, and other violations too numerous to list, investigators never run out of cases. If an investigator took sick leave or vacation, no one picked up the open cases on his or her desk. The piles just kept growing, investigator present or not.

Despite the continued assignment of departmental investigative cases, I felt honored that the Department had enough faith in me and my abilities that they allowed me to take on the additional role. No one said it would be easy or straightforward. But the challenge of this new role provided me some respite from the everyday, routine of internal affairs cases. I continued in both assignments throughout the remainder of 2003 and into 2004 fully supported by the Department's official blessing in assistance rendered to New Mexico.

Only vaguely familiar with John Miller, alias Billy the Kid, I decided to immerse myself in whatever known background history there was that had anything to do with Arizona. At the same time, there were documents and stories about the Kid I felt would shed light on different investigative approaches I might take. I visited the Special Collections Branch at the University of Arizona and spent many hours scrutinizing documents in the Maurice Fulton Collection, and I acquired copies of letters from the Governor Lew Wallace Collection from the Indiana Historical Society. I read Billy the Kid books by Pat Garrett, Frederick Nolan, Robert Utley, and many others. I obtained census records from New Mexico and Arizona and searched genealogy records from Ancestry.com.

I spent many off-duty hours analyzing anecdotal stories from Billy's friends, associates, and enemies. Some were sensible, and honesty was evident. Others were ramblings of older pioneers who often confused dates, participants, and locations, producing misperception and error. Then there were some, that were so obvious in their fabrication and embellishment, they added nothing but misdirection to the historical record; they were intended to inflate the storyteller's relevance. Belief in one story, as opposed to another, is nearly always affected by bias. I suppose sorting through the muddle of information and trying to refrain from concluding without involving one's preconceptions are common phenomena experienced by historians and authors, alike. It was undoubtedly difficult for me.

I was new to this type of effort and was overwhelmed by the massive volume of information. The lack of accurate recordation caused me to reevaluate my efforts, and I focused on those stories and documents that I could track, effectively analyze, and reach conclusions on their merit. I performed extensive empirical research and used scientific methodology. Without getting too deep into my methods, I practiced 'falsifiability.' Falsifiability is the capacity for some proposition, statement, theory, or hypothesis to be proven wrong. That capacity is an essential component of the scientific method and hypothesis testing. As an example, the statement, "John Miller was Billy the Kid," is falsifiable because it was possible to contradict the statement with irrefutable facts. I subsequently followed a simple rule of content analysis that the investigator must always begin with the premise that the account is accurate; the given assumption that bias is in favor of the hypothesis until proven false.

I conducted a content analysis of the letters between Billy the Kid and Governor Lew Wallace and of others with whom both Wallace and the Kid communicated. To summarize my findings, there were numerous written segments I recognized as *'sensitivity clusters.'* These clusters contained content that suggested hidden intentions, deception, and not so apparent agendas. I found unique linguistic styles and cognitive traits attributed to the writer that provided ample opportunity for comparison with other documents and writers.

Since John Miller was the primary target of my investigation, I obtained a book describing his personal history as Billy the Kid in hiding, *Whatever Happened to Billy the Kid,* by Helen Airy. I located death certificates for John Miller and his wife, Isadora. Census records were tracked showing the Millers' movements through New Mexico and Arizona. I found statements from friends living near them along with cemetery records for Isadora. I located the application for admission to the Pioneer Home in Prescott, Arizona, internal documents regarding his residence there and John's cemetery records. I examined all in context with how they lived, and information suggested John Miller was Billy the Kid.

I was caught up in the excitement of possibly changing history and proving that Billy the Kid did not die at the hands of Pat Garrett on July 14, 1881. An investigation eventually contributed to the exhumation of John Miller's remains located in the Arizona Pioneer Home Cemetery in Prescott, Arizona on May 19th, 2005. None of those who participated in the endeavor considered the zeal and antagonism demonstrated by so many Billy the Kid supporters. I was oblivious of other agendas in play including those political, financial and ego-driven; political agendas of the two governors of New Mexico and Arizona; financial gain from filmed documentaries; reelection of local officials; and egos of participants. Initially, I intended to conduct a truth-finding and scientific investigation. Instead, the study turned into a three-ringed circus with no ringmaster.

Sederwall had located the workbench on which the Kid purportedly laid after Pat Garrett shot him. Upon examination of the workbench, Sederwall found blood evidence remaining in the wood and crevices and was able to remove samples containing blood. This effort was not considered extraordinary since there were numerous historical instances when scientists removed blood evidence from objects years beyond the date of the first incident. Sederwall believed the blood samples might produce DNA for comparison to the DNA collected from John Miller's remains.

In Sederwall's estimation, exhumations and examinations of Catherine Antrim, the Kid's mother, as well as John Miller, would produce DNA for comparison to DNA from blood samples removed from the workbench. Any combination of a DNA match would put to rest several issues. First, was it the Kid's blood on the workbench? A DNA match with that of Catherine Antrim would prove or disprove that. Second, the DNA from Miller compared to the DNA of Catherine Antrim would conclusively prove or disprove Miller's identity. Sederwall procured the assistance of a DNA laboratory in Dallas, Texas, and we moved forward to excavate both persons, beginning with John Miller because we had historical records of his exact burial location.

Before the exhumation of John Miller's remains, 2005 Arizona Revised Statutes–§36-27 Disinterment-reinternment Permit, had been amended to allow without a permit or court order, disinterment and reinternment of human remains from a cemetery. To legally exhume human remains, one of the following requirements were to be met:

A. Except as otherwise provided by law, a disinterment-reinternment permit is required before a person disinters human remains. The state registrar shall provide a permit to disinter human remains either by a court order issued in this state or by the written consent of the decedent's family member who has the highest priority. The priority is as follows:

1. Spouse of the decedent at the time of death.
2. All adult offspring.
3. Parents.
4. All adult siblings.

5. Any other family member of legal age.

B. A disinterment-reinternment permit is not required if disinterment and reinternment occur in the same cemetery for ordinary relocation or for reasons of internal management of the cemetery.[2]

Since John Miller had no remaining family, relatives could not provide permission to exhume his remains. However, section 'B' of the statute negated the need for a permit or a court order since approval could be granted by the owners of the cemetery, in this case, the Pioneer Home, in Prescott, Arizona. Written consent was given by Jeanine Dyke, Director of the Pioneer Home, to disinter and reinter Miller's remains within the cemetery. Like all of us who participated in the exhumation, she was interested in determining if John Miller was, in fact, Billy the Kid. If so, she intended to move his remains to a more prominent location within the cemetery and change records to reflect John Miller's identity. Our attorney performed a legal review of the statute and determined that Ms. Dyke's actions constituted "internal management of the cemetery." Kurtis Productions provided the funding, and I coordinated the effort with Ms. Dykes.

We began the excavation on May 19th, 2005. Intending to conduct the disinterment using scientific methodology, we obtained the services of a forensic anthropologist from a medical examiner's office, a representative from the DNA laboratory in Texas, a deputy sheriff from Yavapai County Sheriff's Department, and a film crew to document the process. What we expected to be a low-key effort turned out to be a media event with the presence of about 30 or more observers, including Sederwall, Sheriff Sullivan, and me. In a book previously authored by Sederwall, he referenced Miller's exhumation stating that ". . . the State of Arizona exhumed him." I can say without a doubt that the State of Arizona played no part in the excavation efforts except that we received permission from a subdivision of state government.

Consequently, some level higher than Jeanine Dyke, Director of the Arizona State Pioneer Home, probably approved the effort when we received written permission to proceed.

As the excavation ensued, we learned that we had mistakenly landed in the area between two gravesites. We knew that one of the two belonged to Miller because of the mapping we had of his burial. The other grave contained the remains of William Hudspeth. However, over the years, the graves had shifted through regular geologic action, and we were uncertain as to which resting place belonged to John Miller. With the permission of the Pioneer Home on-sight representative, we excavated first the north grave and then the south grave. The anthropologist examined the remains of both and determined the southern gravesite belonged to Miller. Specimens were recovered from his remains and turned over to the representative of the DNA lab for later analysis. Remains of both excavations were reinterred and restored to their original condition. As a closing moment in respect for John Miller, the investigators gathered around his grave to pay our respects. Sederwall commented to the effect that regardless of whether John Miller was Billy the Kid, his legacy got our attention and made a bunch of cops engage him in a final tribute. He made us look.

During the following year, those who participated in the exhumation were notified first by the Prescott Police Department that someone filed complaints against us for "grave robbing." Even though we followed the law to the letter, there were those in the Billy the Kid, die-hard crowd, who felt we had violated some unwritten code of ethics and committed a criminal violation by exhuming John Miller. What started as a misdemeanor complaint was soon elevated to felony status, and a special prosecutor from the Maricopa County Prosecutor's office was appointed to investigate. That got everyone's attention and for some time, not only were we under investigation, but we frequently received death threats and annoying telephone calls, and we were the heinous celebrities in several newspapers.

Eventually, someone with sensibility prevailed, and the special prosecutor dismissed the investigation. The following lukewarm article appeared in the Arizona Republic alerting us we were off the hook. That didn't stop the opposition, though. Steve Sederwall and Sheriff Tom Sullivan litigated a lawsuit in their home state of New Mexico. Though the court ruled against them initially, the New Mexico Court of Appeals overturned the verdict. But that's another story.

No charges for exhumation in Billy the Kid bones case

ASSOCIATED PRESS

PRESCOTT — Prosecutors won't seek charges against two men who exhumed the remains of a man who claimed to be the outlaw Billy the Kid.

Tom Sullivan, former sheriff of Lincoln County, N.M., and Steve Sederwall, former mayor of Capitan, N.M., dug up the bones of John Miller in May 2005. Miller was buried at the state-owned Pioneers' Home Cemetery in Prescott nearly 70 years ago.

"It appears officials in charge of the facility gave permission and the people who were attempting to recover samples of the remains believed they had permission to do so," said Bill FitzGerald, a spokesman for the Maricopa County Attorney's Office, which made the decision not to seek charges.

Sullivan and Sederwall obtained DNA from Miller's remains.

The samples were sent to a Dallas lab to compare Miller's DNA to blood traces taken from a bench that is believed to be the one the Kid's body was placed on after he was shot to death in 1881.

Sullivan and Sederwall have been hunting for the Kid's bones since 2003.

They began their quest in Fort Sumner, N.M., where history says the Kid was buried after then-Lincoln County Sheriff Pat Garrett gunned him down in 1881.

But at least two men, Miller and Ollie "Brushy Bill" Roberts of Texas, claimed prior to their deaths that they were Billy the Kid. Their stories presuppose that Garrett killed the wrong man and lied about it.

After more than a year of fighting to get permission to unearth the Fort Sumner grave, Sullivan and Sederwall dropped their request and decided to begin the process of elimination in Arizona.

They later returned the bones, and Pioneers' Home officials reinterred them in August.

Figure 16. The Arizona Republic, October 24, 2006, p. 10

[1] Tunnell, Dale L. "Report of Investigation: John Miller." translated by Professional Standards Bureau, Arizona Department of corrections, 2003.

[2] "Arizona Disinterment Reinternment Permit." *2005 Arizona Revised Statutes - §36-327*, Arizona Revised Statutes 2005.

CHAPTER 8

The Pretender

ONE OF MANY PROBLEMS associated with researching John Miller is that there was such limited historical documentation supporting the claim that he was Billy the Kid and that he survived being shot by Pat Garrett on July 14, 1881, in Fort Sumner, New Mexico. Documents attributed to John and Isadora Miller were minimal at best. Helen Airy had recorded several interviews about John and Isadora, but they were anecdotal and not actual evidence. Nor were they publicly available. There were no attributable written statements, letters, or any other first-person form of communication that warranted substantial analysis. Also, I could find only two texts written in support of John Miller's claims that contained any information considered evidentiary. Other books included fantasized episodes and authors wrote them more for entertainment than as historical tomes.

The first text was, *"Encounter with the Frontier,"* written by Gary Tietjen in 1969.[1] After studying this text and having numerous conversations with the author, it is my opinion that this was the genesis for the second, more widely known book, *"Whatever Happened to Billy the Kid,"* by Helen Airy published in 1993.[2] So much of what she wrote in her book seemed to have originated from Gary Tietjen, and her interviews of some of the old Ramah, New Mexico, pioneers were a follow-up to what Tietjen had written earlier. Relying on a previous author isn't necessarily a bad thing. However, there is a tendency to accept as gospel, anecdotal information some of these pioneers provided absent supporting evidence. In all fairness to Airy, she mostly printed what she heard without embellishment or personal bias. In contrast, Tietjen must have updated his first work after Airy because he referenced her book in his updated edition. Both texts had many of the same referenced stories.

Some first-hand accounts carry more weight than others due to the established reputation and credibility of the witness. And in most instances, there are no apparent reasons to disbelieve the stories the old-timers told. They related what they remembered and what they believed. In those days, a person's word was his bond, and unless there was something remarkable to refute a story, it was naturally accepted. In the modern age, however, there are methods to separate fact from fiction, and over time, research methods have improved substantially. Unfortunately, letters or recorded testimony are not available for analysis as they were with Billy the Kid. At least he authored correspondences that we can link directly to him. Those letters opened windows into his mind and certainly provided a basis for psychological and physiological investigation.

Without some direct form of verbal communications, we can only rely on anecdotal stories and government records such as death certificates, census records, courthouse records, and such. I was limited to linking timelines with clues and filling in blanks with the pioneer stories. Not an impossible task, but often more demanding and occasionally misleading as the results are not always conclusive. I decided to examine points made in both books previously mentioned but with more emphasis on the text by Helen Airy since much of her content was drawn from the original paperback by Gary Tietjen.

I examined many discrepancies identified in the Airy text and compared them to census records, court records, and research results by other Billy the Kid investigators. Since no writing samples or authored verbal behavior from the two principals, John and Isadora Miller, were available, I examined anatomical and biological anomalies and deferred to established medical and anthropological knowledge. By seeking fact instead of conjecture, I searched for any evidence that could prove that John Miller was Billy the Kid.

Let's begin with a close look at the history of John Miller presented by Helen Airy in her book, "*Whatever Happened to Billy, the Kid?*" John Miller's story begins with Helen Airy describing the departure of John and Isadora Miller from Fort Sumner, New Mexico.

A Faulty Foundation

The most obvious question to me concerned Airy's description of a seminal event involving the raucous and alleged extensive exchange of gunfire between Sheriff Garrett's posse and Billy the Kid seven to eight days before the night of July 14, 1881. Her excerpt reads:

"Isadora later told friends and neighbors that some days before the shootout at Pete Maxwell's house the kid had been wounded and she had taken him to her home in Fort Sumner. She tended to his wounds and hid him between two straw mattresses, which she slid under the bed when officers came looking for him. When he was well enough to travel, the couple fled Fort Sumner and headed towards the village of Las Vegas, where there were friends to help them."[3]

If this shootout occurred, why, in so many accounts of the

Kid's death, has no one ever described this event in this way? Any similar description of this incident is absent from the stories of persons who were present at the time. According to Airy, William Bonney, alias John Miller, was wounded in a shooting some eight days before Garrett's posse arrived in Fort Sumner. She intimated that he was recuperating from wounds he received from these same officers when they were searching Fort Sumner for him. However, by all accounts except hers, Garrett and his posse did not arrive in Fort Sumner eight days before the shooting but on the night of July 14, 1881. Airy reported that John and Isadora departed Fort Sumner a month later, on August 8th. By her time frame, Billy was shot on July 7th, an impossibility because Pat Garrett was still looking for the Kid in Lincoln and White Oaks at that time. Could it be, that's because it never happened? Or was it, as some would suggest, a massive conspiracy to hide the truth.

Even Tietjen stated, "I interviewed Atheling Bond who told me that when Billy the Kid was shot by Pat Garrett, his body was turned over to the Mexican women for burial. They found him still breathing and substituted for his body in the coffin that of a Mexican man who had died the night before. One woman, Isadora, carefully nursed him until he could be taken by night to Milligan's Plaza (later called Reserve) where he recovered. This close call convinced him to leave Lincoln County and to live under an assumed name in a very sparsely settled area, and he and Isadora came to the El Morro Country under the name of John Miller."[4]

Nowhere does there exist any ascribed testimony from either John or Isadora that they were involved in that incident or even the departure from Fort Sumner. No statement from them exists establishing an even remote connection with Lincoln County, New Mexico. We have only third-party recollections of when they arrived in Ramah, New Mexico, and some assertions that some old-timers knew John Miller as Billy the Kid from when they lived in Lincoln County. In a courtroom, this would be considered inadmissible hearsay testimony.

What does exist is only Helen Airy's description of the event. Could she have been told of the incident by the Millers? No, because they were both dead and she was never able to interview them. Millers' adopted son Max may have related the events to her since he alleged his father told him he was Billy the Kid. While a distinct possibility that Maxwell Miller described the information to her, I question why she didn't attribute this description as originating from Max. She didn't receive her information from Tietjen, though she does include many of the details he authored initially. Regardless, there is no record to indicate where she received her information other than to suggest Max was her source. However, once again, there is an anecdotal story loaded with supposition. The delivery of such a narrative made for a great introduction to the John and Isadora Miller saga but appeared to be inaccurate. Since there was no explanation, this becomes a critical marker when we evaluate the claims made by Miller that he was Billy the Kid. It has been my experience that when a story is so questionable, its foundation generally collapses.

There are several other inconsistencies in the information proffered by Helen Airy and had she not relied so heavily on anecdotal information answers might have been available with substantial research to back up her claims. For instance, John and Isadora Miller allegedly appeared before a parish priest by the name of *"Father Barrera"* and asked him to marry them. This event supposedly occurred in the village of Las Vegas, New Mexico, thirty-one days after his shootout with Pat Garrett and posse.[5] An examination of church records from the Santa Fe Archdiocese in New Mexico disclosed that there was no *"Father Barrera"* anywhere in the Archdiocese during that time. There was a *"Father Herrera"* who was a parish priest in the village of Pecos, but no marriage records for John and Isadora exist. The records extend from 1881 through 1916 for both the Santa Fe and the Gallup Archdioceses.

A lack of Archdiocese records does not mean no marriage occurred; possibly officiated by some justice of the peace or official with that authority. But the reference is made explicitly concerning a "parish" priest. Still, I found no other records in support of that claim, and no one claims to have discovered any. However, we will discuss clues leading to Isadora's identity later.

Isadora told friends and neighbors that some days before the shooting at Pete Maxwell's house in Fort Sumner, the posse wounded the Kid and she took him to her home in Fort Sumner, tended his wounds and hid him between two straw mattresses. Allegedly, when officers came looking for him, she slid the 'mattresses' with him in between, under the bed. Records and accounts of persons including Pat Garrett and John Poe indicate that Garrett and his posse arrived in Fort Sumner on the night of July 14th, 1881, and the next day, after burying Billy the Kid, they departed the area because they were afraid of being mobbed by Billy's friends in Fort Sumner. Once again, there are no indications that the officers remained to look for Billy who they believed already buried, nor was there any suggestion that they engaged in a gunfight with Billy before that date.

The Drive to Ramah

I do not wish to intimate that Helen Airy lied to the reader in this instance or any other. Since her book consisted of nearly all anecdotal stories, she could have received this information from Max Miller, the adopted son of John and Isadora.

According to Airy, he was the first to provide some background regarding the flight from Fort Sumner. I did find it strange that this trek included the care of horses and "milk cows," traveling only at night and hiding out during the day. From my own youthful experiences, I am aware that trailing cattle during the day is difficult at best, let alone trying to move even two of them at night. And for you city folks, milk cows are cattle.[6]

Another interesting discussion suggested that the Millers traveled New Mexico from Las Vegas to Reserve by way of El Morro and back to the Zuni mountains. Miller purportedly reached an agreement with Jesus Eriacho, promising they would look after Eriacho's herd on the Zuni range during the winter for the next five years. Eriacho would share with him the calves born in the spring. After five years the herd would have doubled, providing Miller with a cowherd of his own.

There was a recorded document between John Miller and Jesus Eriacho that spelled out the terms of this agreement. It may not have been the first agreement between the two, but it was the only one recorded. The deal was a cattle contract between Jesus Eriacho and John Miller, dated November 1, 1909, some eighteen years after they supposedly arrived in Ramah, New Mexico. Eriacho agreed to deliver one bull, twelve steers, and thirty-seven cows to Miller in exchange for Miller's ranch property and one dollar. Miller promised to care for the cattle at his expense and pay taxes on these cattle for five years. At the expiration and full performance of the contract, Miller was to deliver one hundred head of healthy animals to include two bulls, twenty-four steers, and seventy-four cows in ages ranging from one year to five years. In the event Miller defaulted on the agreement, he was to return the cattle Eriacho gave him with identifying brands. As a guarantee that Miller would faithfully execute the contract, Miller agreed to sign over all his rights and title to his homestead in the event he failed to comply fully with the requirements of the contract.[7]

It's somewhat comical that John Miller did not own his property at the time they recorded the deal. He did not gain his patent under the Homestead Act until April 29th, 1914. Six days later, John Miller quitclaimed his homestead to Isadora Miller for the sum of one dollar. The action is significant for a couple of reasons. First, it is unknown whether John Miller consummated his contract with Jesus Eriacho, but if he did not, the homestead was to be repossessed by Eriacho in November of 1914. By this time, Miller would have received the patent on his homestead from the General Land Office, and he would have had to turn it over.[8] In somewhat of a smooth move, Miller prevented Eriacho from repossessing his land. Had Isadora and John been officially married, this quitclaim would have been irrelevant. Eriacho would still have been able to gain ownership. Secondly, if on the other hand, John and Isadora were not officially married, the transfer of ownership may have been preventative. Remember that when Miller pledged the property, John didn't own it, the government did. Pursuing civil action, Eriacho might have been able to gain possession anyway, but court battles were most often the exception, not the rule. In short, John pulled a fast one on Eriacho. So much for trusted friends.[9]

Even though cattle contracts were conventional in those days, could it be that the one Airy referred to didn't work out so well, and Eriacho determined that he needed to reduce any future contracts to writing? Or is this recorded contract the one she referred to initially?

The journey John and Isadora made, consisted of nearly 580 miles, pushing milk cows and horses pulling a wagon loaded with supplies. With water stops and feed, rest periods for both animals and the Millers, they could only travel 2 to 3 miles per hour or around 10 miles per day before they had to stop. The trip probably took approximately sixty days, including the layovers in Reserve and Quemado, New Mexico. By the time they arrived in Zuni country, the onset of winter was beginning. Airy's account rings true as to the season of their arrival. In all this description, no one has provided an authenticated date of their arrival in Western New Mexico. The lack of an arrival timeframe brings the trip into question. Could they have arrived in late 1881 or even as late as 1886? No one seems to be able to account for John and Isadora's arrival. People just took it for granted that they came on the scene within a few months after Garrett shot Billy the Kid. I, for one, questioned that supposition.[10]

A Matrimonial Union

This critical question has some bearing on the validity of their account regarding their departure from Fort Sumner, arrival in Las Vegas and even their marriage date and location. Ironically, the information provided in the United States Census of 1900 by both John and Isadora indicated they married in 1886, and both suggested that the marriage existed for 14 years. Was this an inadvertent disclosure on their part? We know that in other census records, they masked many of their demographics. However, they were both consistent about the birth year of their adopted Navajo son, Max and that he was approximately two years of age when they took him in. If the date of their marriage was 1886, then much of their story about their journey to Las Vegas and Isadora caring for John was probably not factual.

Herman Tecklenburg

Another offer of proof regarding John's identity as Billy the Kid was Herman Tecklenburg's story that he knew John Miller during his outlaw days in Fort Sumner and Oklahoma. Tecklenburg said he followed the cattlemen and miners to the western part of the state of New Mexico and was an Indian scout stationed at Fort Wingate, New Mexico, when he again met John Miller. He supposedly knew John Miller when he was working as a cowpuncher around Fort Sumner and was an outlaw known as Billy the Kid. Tecklenburg asserted that the Kid was dodging Pat Garrett and his posse at the time. Using the data provided in the book, I calculated Tecklenburg's age to have been fourteen to sixteen years old at the time he supposedly met Billy the Kid. It's not likely he was on his own during this time, but boys did grow up quickly back then. At any rate, I located no record of the Tecklenburg family in either county records or census records for Lincoln or San Miguel Counties during this timeframe.[11]

Eugene Lambson

The next in the line of Helen Airy interviews was Eugene Lambson. Eugene was three years old when he and his family moved to Ramah, New Mexico. Eugene told Helen Airy that he knew John Miller was Billy the Kid. Eugene did not offer proof except to say that people in the valley knew John Miller was a fugitive and they "thought" John was Billy the Kid. Eugene suggested that John was a good dancer, the same as the Kid. Lambson said Miller talked a lot about the Kid but never admitted that he was the Kid. One night, Lambson went to Miller's place to pick up a horse for his father. He was with another person who he did not identify but stated when they rode up to the Miller Place on their horses, ". . . the dog started barking; John Miller came out the door of the house with a 30-30 rifle pointed at us." They stayed the night and listened to Miller's stories about Billy the Kid, and gunfighters. Miller allegedly showed "the boys" seven scars on his legs from bullet wounds.[12] Historical records suggest that Billy the Kid was shot only twice, once in the upper thigh from a bullet he received from Billy Matthews during the five-day battle in Lincoln and a minor wound on the shoulder from an injury at Blazer's Mill. Some say he received as many as five wounds, but still not the number suggested by Lambson.

Miller told Lambson his wife Isadora and son Max had gone to El Paso for supplies. Lambson insisted the story was accurate and that this trip was made at least once a year, always at night, and sometimes John went with them. It seems strange that they would travel over 700 miles round trip, for supplies, when it was about one-third the distance to and from Albuquerque. Lambson was relying on what Miller told him, but he couldn't have known for sure of the destination or the actual length of time they were gone. Maybe these trips were much shorter and for some other reason. Was this a way for John to appease Isadora's homesickness?

Eugene Lambson said that he and his family left Ramah in 1935, but he returned in 1945 to open a malt and sandwich shop. Lambson said, "One day, a stranger from Phoenix, Arizona, walked into the malt shop. He was looking for an heir to John Miller's estate. He told me John Miller had died in Buckeye, Arizona, and since no one there knew of any survivors, the court-appointed three men to go through his effects but the man said he was one of the persons so appointed, and when they searched through the contents of an old trunk, they found documents, letters, and other items which convinced them John Miller was Billy the Kid."[13]

Lambson's recollection is curious since later Airy wrote that a friend of Miller's when he lived in Buckeye, Carl Baxter, described the events of the Miller housefire in which Isadora had died. Baxter said when the Miller house caught fire, young Carl Baxter helped carry Isadore's body from the burning building. "She was a corpse," Baxter said, "but she wasn't burned." Baxter thinks she may have died before the fire started. His account is questionable since Isadora's death certificate says otherwise.[14]

Isadora's Death and the Mysterious Trunk

On Isadora's death certificate dated October 18, 1936, the attending physician stated, "I saw a burned and charred body and believe from witnesses at hand that said the body was that of Dora Miller, who burned to death when her house burned."[15]

Baxter added that he remembered the old humpback trunk next to the Miller fireplace, covered with an Indian blanket.

"You had to be very close to Miller to get near the trunk," Baxter said, "Miller kept his guns in there, and some photographs, keepsakes, and papers. He showed me a pistol with 21 notches, some ammunition, old cartridges, a Buffalo gun, pictures, and a slug he dug out of his body with a pocketknife. And he showed me a ceramic jar with a lid on it that he kept in the bottom of the trunk that was filled with gold and silver coins."[16]

Baxter said, "After the fire, I was helping to clean up the burned building, and we found a patch of melted gold coins on the floor where the old trunk stood-about half a teacup full of melted gold."[17]

Baxter does not know what happened to the trunk, the guns it held, or the rest of the coins and keepsakes. So far as Baxter knows, Miller did not save any possessions from the fire. His statement suggests there was no trunk after the blaze. And considering the inconsistency between Isadora's death certificate and Baxter's account of her death, his story about John's chest is somewhat questionable. However, Baxter said that the night before the fire, Miller had been up all night "wandering about." He surmised that it is probable that the trunk was hidden and retrieved by Miller, and when he died, someone found it and turned over to the court authorities in Phoenix. A representative of the court may have then taken the trunk to Ramah, where Eugene Lambson reported the representative of the Phoenix court walked into his sandwich shop and asked Lambson to direct him to the heir of John Miller's estate.[18] And of course, this episode occurred in 1945, some eight years after John Miller's death. Do you think a probate court would wait eight years to search for an heir to an estate that consisted of a trunk containing some relics, documents, and photos?

The Probate Mystery

It's interesting to note that while Isadora Miller did die that night in a little village of Liberty, near Buckeye, John Miller died in Prescott, Arizona, slightly over a year later. He had no possessions at the time of his death. An extensive search of the Phoenix Probate Court archives revealed no records of any property belonging to John Miller of Liberty or Prescott, Arizona. The same was true of any files existing in Yavapai County. A similar search of the records at the Arizona State Archives also turned up nothing.

This entire story has several flaws in it, beyond the absence of records. First, if a trunk were discovered after the fire, containing papers and documents identifying John Miller as Billy the Kid, the contents would have probably found their way to the media. Considering the notoriety of Billy the Kid, the finder would have been famous. No disclosure happened. But let's say, the finder was honest. The next thing to occur would have been to turn over the property to the Maricopa County Sheriff for disposal as found property, not the Probate Court. Suppose the trunk somehow ended up in probate. This occurrence would have been highly unusual since this would have necessitated that first, the minimum value of the chest and contents had to be over $2500 for that time.

Secondly, for court action to occur, someone would have had to file a petition for probate in John Miller's name. Then, if the property were in probate, there would have been a notice placed in the local newspapers to heirs of the John Miller estate. If the court located an heir, a letter would have been sent, directing the heir to file a claim and appear before the court to take possession of the property. A significant document trail would exist. And finally, the court does not send representatives on the road with the property, in search of heirs, especially out of state. Considering limited resources, the Probate Court wouldn't have assigned representatives to physically travel to New Mexico in search of an heir they did not know for sure even existed, much less wait eight years to initiate a search. And all the while, we are to rely on a belief that a bureaucrat of the probate court was honest enough to carry through the search for John Miller's heirs knowing what the trunk contained.

Having searched for the elusive trunk myself, I was informed by people who knew Max Miller, John's adopted son, that he had received the chest in question, though he said to Helen Airy he knew nothing about it. He allegedly handed it down through his family, and it rested at some undisclosed location on the Navajo Reservation. Wouldn't one think that if Max had the trunk with all this proof, that he would have presented it to someone in support of the story that his adopted father was, in fact, Billy the Kid? That never happened. To the extent Max believed his father was Billy the Kid, this would have become the primary point of proof. Doesn't it also seem convenient and add to the John Miller mystique that this trunk contained "*papers and photographs*" proving John Miller was Billy the Kid, yet it somehow disappeared from history? Knowing that there were first-hand accounts of the trunk's existence before the Liberty fire, I believe that unless someone produces the chest, it didn't exist after the house fire.

Too Many Wounds

Next, a young man by the name of Atheling Bond said he knew John Miller and believed him to be Billy the Kid because Miller's wife, Isadora, and son, Max told him so. His story was in addition to claims made by Herman Tecklenburg. He said that even if he had not heard the stories about Miller, Bond would have known that Miller was the Kid because of the way Miller, "told stories as if he were doing it himself." Bond said,

"John Miller liked to tell stories about Billy the Kid's gunfights, but he did not want us to think he, himself, was the Kid. He would end each story about the Kid's adventures by reminding us that he was not Billy the Kid. However, his wife Isadora who could not speak English, would tell us in Spanish that he really was Billy the Kid and his name was not John Miller. She told us how Billy was shot in Fort Sumner, and how she took care of his wounds, and when the officers came around to her house looking for him, she hid him between two straw mattresses which she slid under the bed."[19]

Is this the source of the original story presented by Helen Airy? Airy avoided ever suggesting any of this was fact, but she continued the narrative anyway, weaving what she believed was a compelling story.

One especially exciting account by Bond was that one night he and Rulon Ashcroft stayed overnight with John Miller. After supper, Miller started telling stories about Billy the Kid, and after a while, took off his shirt and showed the boys where there were twelve bullet holes in his body. Where the shots

came out, there was supposedly a spot about the size of a silver dollar. And where they went in, they were about the size of a little finger. Now, remember, this was a period when medical cures were still rudimental, and there was a lack of skilled physicians. They were using poultices of cow manure on open wounds. It was highly effective for drawing out infection and thorns, but can you imagine the bacteria entering an open wound?[20]

At any rate, twelve bullet wounds striking the chest and exiting the back would be extreme trauma to the torso, and even if one didn't die of shock immediately, they would have bled out. Not only considering extensive damage to vital organs, but the odds that so many bullet wounds would not have struck bone is also beyond comprehension.

The boys were young, and Miller took advantage of their gullibility. The story is beyond believability. It is more likely that these scars were the result of serious diseases such as septicemia or blood poisoning. When the bacteria (no doubt aided by cow manure poultices) that causes sepsis, invades the bloodstream, they produce toxins (poisons) that attack the lining of the blood vessels, so the blood vessels begin to leak. This leakage causes a rash of septicemia, which can rapidly develop into larger purple areas of skin. This leakage of blood means that there is not enough blood to carry oxygen to all parts of the body. At the same time, the toxins cause blood clots to form in the tiny blood vessels in the skin, making it even harder for blood to reach all parts of the body. The circulatory system reduces the blood supply to the extremities such as the hands, feet and the surface of the skin to maintain circulation to the vital organs (the brain, liver, kidneys, heart, and lungs).

When skin loses blood supply, starvation of oxygen and essential nutrients occurs, and patches of it die off and blacken.

Nasty cases of septicemia can leave skin scars and more profound damage to muscle and bone. They would resemble bullet exit wounds.

A Rapid Departure

Another thought-provoking disclosure involved testimony by Feliz Bustamante. She lived with the Millers during her childhood. She said that there was an argument "over nothing" between her father-in-law, Solomon Dias and Isadora Miller. What relevance did her living with the Millers in her childhood have to do with the incident between Dias and Isadora? She certainly was not a child during this exchange because by the time of the argument, she was married to Solomon Dias's son. Maybe her closeness to the Millers adds some degree of credibility, but that Airy did not explain. Regardless of what the argument was about, Bustamante said that it caused the Millers to load up the wagon with their belongings and immediately depart their ranch. She said, "They left everything. They just took their possessions and supplies and corn for the team. They left all the cattle, horses, chickens—everything, and I never saw them again."[21]

Earlier in the book, however, Miller is described as taking his time gathering supplies and preparing for their trip to Arizona. Something is amiss. Since Bustamante remembered this episode, it has some import. The argument between Dias and Isadora must have added to the spontaneity of their departure. Maybe Bustamante exaggerated the importance of the disagreement, but I believe there was more to it. Possibly, Diaz knew something about Isadora that Isadora did not want to disclose, and she had a past that may explain the importance of the exchange.

Of course, this may be conjecture on my part. The fact that the Millers didn't take their farm animals with them could mean that someone repossessed the livestock, poultry, and the farm before their departure. Times were hard then and the Millers, like so many others of their ilk, were probably in debt and without further means to earn a living.

The Ontario Provincial Police Inspector

Then there is the story provided by Frank Burrard "Bert" Creasy. Helen Airy took Creasy's story nearly verbatim from an interview he gave in 1979 and included it in her book.[22] Creasy was a retired district inspector of the Ontario Provincial Police in Canada, and he was eighty-eight when interviewed. I have included his account verbatim as it provides a sound basis for some other issues. His account reads as follows:

"I left England in 1906 and jumped ship at New York. I was 16 years old when I first headed west and went looking for a cousin that I understood could be found at an Indian trading post near Ramah, New Mexico. It was while I was working at the trading post that I first met John Miller when he came in for supplies.

"I worked for John Miller for a year and a half, on and off, before I learned that he was in reality, Billy the Kid (William Bonney.)

"It was while we were coming back from a horse drive and had stopped in at a town for a few drinks that I first learned of his true identity. He didn't get to town too often, and when he did, he made the most of it. After telling me, he made me promise not to tell anyone his true identity until after he had passed away. The west was full of tough cowboys eager to make an easy reputation.

"In 1916 I left New Mexico and enlisted with the British Recruiting Mission in Kansas City. They shipped me off to Toronto where I completed my training with the RCDs at Stanley Barracks before going overseas.

"When I came back from the war, I joined the Welland City Police Force and remained there until 1921 when I joined up with the OPP (Ontario Provincial Police) from which I retired in 1958 as a senior staff inspector.

"The following is an actual account of Billy the Kid as I know it.

"William H. Bonney was born in 1859 in Coffeyville, Kansas. He was three years old when his father died, and in 1864 his mother remarried to a Mr. Antrim and the family then moved to Santa Fe and two years later moved again, this time to Silver City.

"The first time anyone really heard of the name Billy the Kid was in 1871 when he was 12 years old. A deputy sheriff apparently insulted Billy's mother for which Billy promptly shot him and then fled to the hills.

"He made his next appearance in Arizona four years later in 1875 when he killed another man in a gunfight and later had a shootout with three Indians and a white man over a dispute in a horse-trading deal. He killed all four.

"He made his next appearance in New Mexico during the famous Cattle War of the West, where he was arrested and thrown into the Lincoln jail from which he escaped his guard and a deputy sheriff in the process.

"He was now declared an outlaw and a reward of $10,000 was put on his head, dead or alive so the wanted posters read.

"He did not show up again until 1880 when at the age of 21, he returned to Lincoln to visit his Mexican sweetheart. He was at that time in the company of an Indian boy who was of about the same age and build.

"Hearing that a cow had been butchered and one of the sides of beef hung next door, the Indian stole over later that night to remove part of the meat for dinner the next day.

"Pat Garrett who was the marshal of Lincoln at the time, and a well-known bounty hunter, heard that Bill was in town and along with two of his deputies laid in waiting near the side of beef.

"When the Indian boy stepped up onto the veranda of the house, he was shot down by Pat Garrett who had apparently mistaken him for Billy. Billy told me once that he and the Indian were dressed alike to confuse people.

"Pat Garrett was later killed in a gunfight with an outlaw by the name of Brazel at Las Cruces in 1909, but he did collect the reward for Bill the Kid of $10,000.

"Billy was not heard of again until 1902 when he and six others held up a bank somewhere in Montana and got away with $8,000. The money was soon hidden in two different locations, $4,000 at each spot.

"The posse, however, closed in on them and five were shot and two got away one of which was Jesus Cacouse who I later knew personally. Billy was badly wounded in the side and had to be seared with a red-hot branding iron to stop the bleeding. I saw the scar of this wound myself. Billy stood trial and bought his pardon for $4,000 and I saw this pardon many times after it was framed and hung on the wall of Billy's ranch house. It was under the name of John Miller.

"Billy then settled down and homesteaded twenty-five miles south of Ramah, New Mexico where he raised horses. While I worked at his ranch I remember three different occasions when the sale of horses would fall off and money got scarce and shortly John Miller would disappear with his old friend and return in two or three weeks with saddlebags filled with gold coins in five, ten, and twenty-dollar denominations.

"I helped him wash the dirt off these coins and was paid my wages with some of this gold and often had an extra $20 gold piece thrown in for good measure.

"Billy often told me bits and pieces of his past life while we were out on the trail delivering horses to the various cattle ranches, and when I left to join up in World War I, old John gave me the gun and belt that I now have in my possession.

"In 1932 or 33 I received a letter from my cousin in Ramah where I first met Billy Bonney, alias John Miller, Billy the Kid. My cousin, Bob Masters said that the Kid had sold his ranch and bought another at the head of Horse Head Canyon and that after a few years he had died at the age of 73. I was then living at Haileybury and serving as a senior staff inspector in charge of the district OPP."[23]

That was quite a story. Three things to consider about Creasy's account before looking further into the details. First, Creasy was sixteen or seventeen when John Miller provided this information. Second, there was liquor involved. And third, he was eighty-eight years old when he granted this interview. Those three issues will account for some of the discrepancies apparent in this narrative. Youth and liquor at the time of telling and old age at the time of recounting all contribute to confusion and misinformation. But those things don't account for all of the inconsistencies.

Now, I don't doubt that John Miller provided a good deal of the story, so insinuation that Frank Creasy lied about any of this is not intentional. However, there is ample documentation to contest the entire description Creasy provided about Billy's early years.

CHAPTER 8: THE PRETENDER | 143

"William H. Bonney was born in 1859 in Coffeyville, Kansas. He was three years old when his father died, and in 1864 his mother remarried to a Mr. Antrim and the family then moved to Santa Fe and two years later moved again, this time to Silver City. The first time anyone really heard of the name Billy the Kid was in 1871 when he was 12 years old. A deputy sheriff apparently insulted Billy's mother for which Billy promptly shot him and then fled to the hills."[24]

Including Billy's year of birth, historians discredited the preceding account. William McCarty's life did not begin in Coffeyville, Kansas. There is ample documentation that William Antrim accompanied Catherine, Henry, and Joseph to Wichita, Kansas, from Indianapolis. Their departure from Wichita may have been due to Catherine's tuberculosis. They moved first to Colorado and then to Santa Fe, New Mexico where Catherine McCarty married William Antrim in 1873. Church records identify the marriage date and the presence of Henry and Joseph as witnesses. From there they traveled to Silver City, New Mexico where Billy's mother died in 1874. No record exists detailing Billy's shooting of a deputy sheriff in Silver City though only rumored so, and the suggestion that the first time anyone heard of the name, Billy the Kid, was in 1871 is undoubtedly mischaracterized.

So, one might ask, "Where did this information originate?" There are so many glaring holes in this story that it's a waste of effort to describe them all. When one examines the details Creasy provided, it is relatively easy to determine their origin. One needs to look no further than Pat Garrett's *The Authentic Life of Billy the Kid*.[25] Ghostwritten by Ash Upson, the basis of Creasy's description of Billy's early life has been refuted and discounted by authors such as Robert Utley, Frederick Nolan, Leon Metz, and others. It's nothing more than an inaccurate portrayal of Billy's early life exaggerated by Ash

Upson in Pat Garrett's book. Most of what Creasy presented is utter nonsense, except that he believed the story as presented to him by John Miller.

There is an argument to be made, though not a very good one, that John Miller's account to Creasy was correct and based on his own experience. However, since much of the information was made up by Upson and Garrett and later discredited, John Miller was not speaking from experience, but from what he read or from what he learned from others. Remember that Garrett's book was written in 1882 and was available for any-one to read for twenty-four years by the time, John regaled young Creasy with his tales. Creasy wasn't the only individual duped by this fabrication. Pat Garrett's inaccurate accounting was also reiterated in, *The Saga of Billy the Kid,* by Walter Noble Burns[26] and, *History of Billy the Kid,* by Charles Siringo,[27] and others, all the while, presented as fact.

There is another issue with Creasy's remanences that is bothersome; the story about John Miller's pardon from the State of Montana, for bank robbery. Creasy's explanation introduces an intriguing twist in the saga of John Miller.

Explicitly, Creasy stated, "Billy was not heard of again until 1902 when he and six others held up a bank somewhere in Montana and got away with $8,000. The money was soon hidden in two different locations, $4,000 at each spot.

"The posse, however, closed in on them and five were shot and two got away, one of which was Jesus Cacouse who I later knew personally. Billy was badly wounded in the side and had to be seared with a red-hot branding iron to stop the bleeding. I saw the scar of this wound myself. Billy stood trial and bought his pardon for $4,000, and I saw this pardon many times after it was framed and hung on the wall of Billy's ranch house. It was under the name of John Miller."[28]

First, Creasy did not have first-hand knowledge of John Miller's disappearance until 1902, since Creasy was still in England. He didn't arrive in Ramah, New Mexico until 1906. So, where did this story originate? It was probably another tale generated by John Miller. Creasy may have observed the pardon hanging on the wall as he did describe it with some commitment. However, searching the Montana State Historical Society and several records repositories, I was unable to locate a pardon for this John Miller. There were Territorial Prison records for another John Miller, and that John Miller did in fact, receive executive clemency in that timeframe. But it was for horse theft, not a bank robbery. And that John Miller had a history of horse theft in Idaho and Western Montana. That certainly doesn't mean the pardon for our John Miller doesn't exist. Maybe it hides among old mildewed documents in the collections of Montana history. The story behind the clemency is intriguing since it resembles an incident and a series of events in Montana during that time that had nothing to do with John Miller. More on that later.

Second, Billy the Kid was not killed in Lincoln, New Mexico, while visiting his Mexican girlfriend. Purportedly, Garrett shot and killed him in Fort Sumner. Third, this did not happen in 1880, but in 1881.

Fourth, Creasy also said, "Pat Garrett was later killed in a gunfight with an outlaw by the name of Brazel at Las Cruces in 1909, but he did collect the reward for Billy the Kid of $10,000." Once again, John Miller could not have told him this since the incident of Garrett's death occurred after Creasy no longer worked for Miller after 1907. It's possible, Miller relayed the information to him while Creasy worked at his cousin's trading post, but Miller did not impart that knowledge the night of the trail drive.

Fifth, there never was a reward posted for Billy for $10,000.

Governor Lew Wallace posted an award of $1,000 in general for the arrest of rustlers and lawbreakers in Lincoln County. The only reward posted for Billy the Kid was for $500 after he killed Deputies Olinger and Bell when he broke jail in Lincoln. While Garrett had some difficulty collecting the reward, I believe he was finally able to collect it but only through territorial legislative action.

Sixth, in all my research, I could find no reference to an Indian boy in Billy's company except as possibly falsely presented by Miller to Creasy. When John Poe remarked to Pat Garrett that he had killed the wrong person, it was in part because he didn't believe Billy was foolish enough to be in Fort Sumner and partly because Billy spoke Spanish when he confronted Poe and Pete Maxwell.

Seventh, Creasy also said that Miller told him he and the Indian were dressed alike to confuse people. This comment seems doubtful since not only was Billy already recognized by most people in Fort Sumner, but Pat Garrett also knew him. And then there is the question, why would someone dress like Billy considering the possibility that as a Billy the Kid lookalike, they faced a limited future? Remember, it didn't work so well for Charlie Bowdre when the posse mistakenly killed him at Stinking Springs, just for wearing a hat that at a distance made him look like Billy.

How could a well-respected law enforcement officer have gotten so many details wrong? As I stated earlier, a combination of youth, liquor, and old age, fashioned a tremendous-sounding tale. By the time the correspondent interviewed Creasy at the age of eighty-eight, his memory might have been affected somewhat by what he read about Billy over seventy years. Or it was merely a case of John Miller providing him with a false narrative.

Gary Tietjen once wrote in his book, *Encounter with the*

Frontier: "The outlaws I knew were not noted for truthfulness and it is quite possible they told their story differently each time."[29]

Another interesting point in Helen Airy's book is that the author paid very little attention to the background of Isadora Miller. Though census records existed in 1900 and 1910 that identified John and Isadora Miller in the Ramah country, their ages, dates of birth, heritage and other demographic data changed somewhat randomly. I believe they attempted to disguise their true identities for some perceived fear of being caught. However, they occasionally slipped and inadvertently disclosed information that would lead an investigator to a determination of their identities. Nothing in the census records provided conclusive evidence. Nonetheless, when added to documents discovered many years later, a clearer picture evolves.

Who Was Isadora Miller?

One important document provides a simple clue otherwise overlooked by many, including Helen Airy. It might be Airy didn't have the access, or she ignored it. I mentioned the document earlier to dispute the claim by Carl Baxter that Isadora Miller was not burned in the fire that took her life. The record is from the Arizona State Department of Health; Standard Certificate of Death, #F3150657.[30] So, what was the clue?

In items 12–16, the death certificate disclosed Dora's birthplace, her father's name, mother's name, and their place of birth. Her husband, John, provided this information. He listed her place of birth as Las Vegas, New Mexico, and her father's name was "Sise." This spelling is an anglicized version of the Mexican name of "Sais" or "Saiz." Remember also, that in the 1900 U.S. Census, Isadora Miller stated she had no living children. However, in the 1910 U.S. Census, she said she had borne two children, one still living. She could not have been referring to her adopted son Max because the census question asks sequentially, "Number of Children Born," and "Number of Children Living." In the 1900 census, she stated her date of birth was December 1849. Of course, to sow confusion, she changed her year of birth again in the 1910 census to 1852.

An exhaustive search of the New Mexico Hispanic Genealogical Research Center revealed some stimulating information. Isadora Saiz (Sise) was born in 1849. On May 25, 1867, she married Jose Pedro Padilla in the San Jose Church, Anton Chico, New Mexico. Her father was Manuel Antonio Saiz, and her mother was Maria Marcelena Gutierrez. She had both an older brother, Juan Saiz and an older sister, Maria Delores Saiz. Sometime before February 10, 1868, her son, Jose Padilla Padilla (same middle name and last name) was born. A year later, on or before February 10, 1869, her daughter, Maria Antonia Padilla was born. They christened both children in the same church in Anton Chico, New Mexico.

At some point in the next three years, both her husband and son perished with no reason provided. Then, on January 14, 1870, she married Cesario Gurule in the same church in Anton Chico, New Mexico. At the same time, Cesario adopted Isadora's daughter, and she became Maria Antonia Gurule shortened to Antonia Gurule. She was two years old.

Isadora was just eighteen years old when she married Jose and losing him and her son a short time later must have been excruciating for her. Now she was an approximately 21-year-old widow with a young daughter to raise. Meeting Cesario may have been a blessing or a disaster; we may never know. Is it possible that Isadora grew tired of life with Cesario and leaving her child behind, ran off with a man calling himself John Miller? Since both provided census information that their marriage began in 1886 and both stated they had been married for fourteen years, it might be that they were never really married, since no one has located a matrimonial record. If this is so, Isadora departed with John Miller and left behind a daughter of seventeen or eighteen, possibly married by this time and starting a family of her own.

I think it's also possible that the argument Isadora had with Solomon Diaz may have had something to do with her real identity and her need to remain free of her true husband, Cesario. Once again, it is purely my conjecture that I reach this conclusion, but hey . . . it makes for a great story.

No matter how one views the narratives proffered in Helen Airy's book, *Whatever Happened to Billy the Kid,* one thing remains above all else. John and Isadora Miller were pioneers of the West. They survived harsh winters, drought, pestilence, disease, poverty, and a thousand other impediments to a good life. That should have been their real story. It is somewhat sad that their legitimate historical contribution has been overshadowed by those who prefer fallacy over fact. The chronicle of John and Isadora Miller lacks veracity. But is that proof John Miller was not Billy the Kid? No, it is not. After perusing and researching the allegations made here, a reader might conclude that there was not enough evidence to argue against his claim. In other words, I may not have presented a line of reasoning substantial enough to legitimately justify a counter conclusion.

Assessment of information relies on many processes that include reasoning, critical thinking, and understanding. Throughout Airy's book, John Miller denied more times than not, that he was Billy the Kid. But in the end, the result may boil down to forming a humble opinion. When that occurs, it becomes necessary to introduce the fact that becomes indisputable. So, let's do that now

[1] Tietjen, G.L. *Encounter with the Frontier.* 1969.

[2] Airy, Helen. *Whatever Happened to Billy the Kid?* 1st edition, Sunstone Press, 1993.

[3] Ibid. (pp. 9-10)

[4] Tietjen, G.L. *Encounter with the Frontier.* 1969. (p. 58)

[5] Airy, Helen. *Whatever Happened to Billy the Kid?* 1st edition, Sunstone Press, 1993. (p.9)

[6] Ibid. (pp. 11-15)

[7] Eriacho, Jesus and John Miller. "Cattle Contract." Contract, 1909.

[8] America, United States of and John Miller. "Patent." edited by General Land Office, 1914.

[9] Miller, John and Isadora Miller. "Quitclaim." 1914.

[10] Airy, Helen. *Whatever Happened to Billy the Kid?* 1st edition, Sunstone Press, 1993. (pp.11-15)

[11] Ibid.(pp. 42-46)

[12] Ibid. (pp. 48-49)

[13] Ibid. (pp.140-141)

[14] Ibid. (p. 140)

[15] Arizona, State of. "Standard Certificate of Death of Dora Miller." edited by Arizona State Board of Health, 1936.

[16] Airy, Helen. *Whatever Happened to Billy the Kid?* 1st edition, Sunstone Press, 1993. (p. 140)

[17] Ibid. (p. 140)

[18] Ibid. (p. 141)

[19] Ibid. (p. 57)

[20] Ibid. (p. 57)

[21] Ibid. (p. 134)

[22] Ibid. (pp. 90-95)

[23] Creasy, Frank. "Frank Creasy Reminisces." *The O.P.P. Review*, vol. 14, no. 2, 1979, pp. 8,9.

[24] Ibid.

[25] Garrett, Pat F. *The Authentic Life of Billy, the Kid, the Noted Desperado of the Southwest, Whose Deeds of Daring and Blood Made His Name a Terror in New Mexico, Arizona and Northern Mexico.* New Mexican printing and publishing co., 1882.

[26] Burns, Walter Noble. *The Saga of Billy the Kid.* Doubleday, Page & Company, 1926.

[27] Siringo, Charles A. *History of "Billy the Kid,".* 1920.

[28] Creasy, Frank. "Frank Creasy Reminisces." *The O.P.P. Review*, vol. 14, no. 2, 1979, pp. 8,9.

[29] Tietjen, G.L. *Encounter with the Frontier.* 1969. (p. 59)

[30] Arizona, State of. "Standard Certificate of Death of Dora Miller." edited by Arizona State Board of Health, 1936.

CHAPTER 9

Imposter Unmasked

WHEN I DESCRIBED BILLY the Kid's anatomy earlier, I drew your attention to several features based on scientific research. Unambiguously, I described the uniqueness of Billy's anatomy. These include:

- Ears
- Ptosis of his eyelids
- Asymmetric features of his face
- Protrusion of his upper teeth and a small mouth
- Arching of his eyebrows
- *Rounding* and sloping of his shoulders

When one compares the tintype photograph of Billy the Kid to pictures of John Miller, none of these features match. A direct comparison of Billy's right ear to that of John Miller is enough to draw a definitive conclusion. Billy's right ear appears to be cropped or squared with almost no lobe. The ear is protrusive, and the concha seems to be triangular.

John displayed elongated ear lobes. Both ears were situated closer to his head and not protrusive, except his hat made it look so. The concha formed a narrower channel, and his lobes appeared long and unattached to the facial skin. John did not display ptosis, and his eyebrows were flat. His face was

*Figure 17. William H. Bonney alias Billy the Kid
(Photographer Ben Wittick (1845–1903).) Public domain.*

symmetrical, and he presented a full mouth with little or no dental protrusion. And finally, while Billy's neck was short, his shoulders were narrow, rounded and severely sloped. John Miller displayed squared shoulders and a more extended, pronounced neck definition. These features alone should differentiate between the two individuals. The proof is in the details, not photo matching. While John Miller's photo is somewhat blurred, and the outline of the ears are challenging to see, the structure of the shoulder saddle is unmistakable.

A closer examination of the aged John Miller is possible in Helen Airy's book by examining a close-up of a photo owned by Henry Bustamonte or his heirs. But there is more. As a final effort in the investigation of John Miller's claim that he was Billy the Kid as described earlier, a team unearthed John Miller's remains in May 2005.

In Helen Airy's book, she quoted Max Miller as saying, "My parents moved to Buckeye, Arizona because the Old Man said there were hot springs there that would help his rheumatism. My mother smoked cigarettes and was smoking in bed and set the house on fire and died. Then the Old Man was by himself. I wrote and told him to come back home, but he wouldn't do it. Then he fell off the roof he was fixing and was hurt, and he wrote and told me to come bring him home."[1]

Miller died at the Arizona State Pioneer Home on November 7, 1937, and the home buried him in the Arizona State Pioneer Home Cemetery, Iron Springs Road, Prescott, Arizona.

What was crucial to making a proper identification of John Miller's remains was Max's reference to Miller falling off a roof and hurting himself. The attending physician's remarks on Miller's death certificate stated that he attended Miller from October 1937 until the date of his death on November 7, 1937; that he died at 6:30 p.m. The principal cause of death and related causes of importance were as follows: Fractured femur and bronchial pneumonia.[2]

Forensic Anthropologist, Dr. Laura Fulginiti supervised and performed the examination of remains during the excavation and authored a report to me. She reported on June 2nd, 2005, that, ". . . the gravesite was located using the line of headstones to the West of the target grave. A standard reference point was established as the headstone of Michael Clancy. At approximately 1400 hours, a backhoe began to remove the sod overlying the alleged grave, which oriented in an East-

Figure 18. John Miller about 50 years of age. Reprinted with permission from Anita Liston, daughter and heir to the original owner, Jewel Crocket Lambson. © Anita Liston.

West direction, with the head to the West. When fragments of wood began to be removed, the grave was excavated using a shovel. Once the top of the casket and portion of femur were unearthed, the excavation relied on digging with trowels and by hand. The position of the femur indicated that the remains were supine, with the feet to the East and the skull to the West. The left femoral shaft, minus the head, was removed, examined and packaged for subsequent DNA analysis."

After consulting with cemetery staff and others, I determined that the adjacent grave to the north, was more likely that of Mr. Miller and excavation shifted to that gravesite. However, I was later proven wrong.

Dr. Fulginiti wrote: "The backhoe removed the overlying soil until fragments of wood began to be unearthed. The excavation shifted to shovels and the top of the casket was identified. Excavation proceeded using trowels and hand tools until various aspects of the skeleton were identified and cleared. The skeleton in this grave was also lying supine, head to the West and feet to the East. The casket had collapsed onto the body at some point prior to the exhumation process. A metal detector on loan from the Yavapai County Sheriff's Office . . . was used to locate metal items, including nails and casket fittings. (These items were donated to the Arizona Pioneer Home for their museum.)

"Minimal historical artifacts, such as buttons, a possible rivet, portions of the wood from the casket and casket fittings were identified as they were unearthed. Skeletal elements were measured for depth and location, removed from the grave and examined. Pathological conditions such as osteoarthritis, healed fractures and markers of occupation were noted as follows: The vertebrae exhibited signs of extreme osteoarthritis in the form of lipping of the vertebral bodies, collapse of some of the bodies and osteophytic activity. There were extensive healed traumata on the right scapula and the left clavicle, a healed Colles' fracture of the right distal radius, a healed fracture of the second rib and a healed fracture of the left fourth metacarpal. The bone was dark brown in color, friable and dry. There was postmortem damage, both from the collapse of the lid of the casket onto the remains as well as from the removal process. The remains were photographed, samples were harvested for DNA (tooth and femur), and the remains were returned to the grave and reburied."

Dr. Fulginiti wrote further: "Anecdotal historical information suggested that Mr. John Miller had died from complications of a fractured hip while recuperating at the Arizona

Pioneer Home. The individual in the north grave, while having extensive pathological conditions, particularly in the upper body, did not have discernible pathology of the os coxae (innominate bone, pelvic bone). At this point in the excavation, a decision was made to exhume the os coxae of the individual in the south grave to confirm that we had indeed excavated the remains of Mr. John Miller from the north grave. The south grave was excavated by shovel to the point where the remnants of the casket lid were identified. Excavation resumed using trowels and hand tools until the left femoral head was identified.

"The head of the femur was misshapen with bony remodeling, suggesting an antemortem (prior to death) injury. Additional excavation revealed the left innominate, which also had extensive remodeling of the acetabulum, ischium and pubis. The ischium tapered into a point, with lack of union to the pubis, suggesting a healing fracture of the ischiopubic ramus. This evidence led the team to believe that the individual in the south grave was, in fact, more consistent with the known facts regarding the medical history of Mr. John Miller and additional DNA samples were recovered. The maxillae and mandible were recovered but were edentulous (missing teeth). There was limited pathology of the vertebrae, ribcage, clavicles and scapulae of the individual from the south grave. Mild osteoarthritis of the vertebral bodies was the only pathology of note. Photographs of the cranium and mandible were taken, and the remains were returned to the grave and reburied."[3]

What this report means in plain English is that the individual in the south grave had a severely fractured hip while the person in the north grave did not. We identified the person in the north grave as William Hudspeth, 1869-1937. The south grave contained the remains of John Miller. Note Dr. Fulginiti observed no trauma to the upper torso of John Miller. This finding indicated that John Miller did not receive twelve bullet wounds as claimed by Atheling Bond nor did he receive bullet trauma on either side of his chest from his alleged shootout with Pat Garrett or his deputies. The anthropological evidence demonstrated that John was never wounded as he claimed. The severe wound described by Isadora never happened. John told many folks he wasn't Billy the Kid. They should have listened to him. But then again, legends nearly always outlive the truth.

One final note about John Miller's end-of-life stay in the Arizona State Pioneer Home. John's friend, N.M.J. Mayhan, certified under oath that John was eighty-eight years of age and that he had resided in Arizona continuously for thirty-five plus years and his signature was notarized on December 12, 1936. If according to Helen Airy's book, John and Isadora moved to Arizona in 1917 or 1918 as suggested, he had resided in Arizona for only eighteen to nineteen years at the time he presented this application. Once again, John was able to beat the system. Only this time he defrauded the State of Arizona with free room and board until his death in 1937.[4] John didn't have much choice, though. Nowhere to live and an incapacity to be mobile, the Arizona State Home for Pioneers and Miners was his only alternative. His final year wasn't much of a life, and except for the presence of staff at the Home, John died alone, without friends or relatives. That wasn't much of an epitaph for an old pioneer, even if he lied to get there.

So, if John Miller wasn't Billy the Kid, then who was he? Some incidents occurred up in Montana about the time John Miller surfaced, and they might have some bearing on his identity. Let's have some fun with the next chapter and see if the pieces fit.

---

[1] Airy, Helen. *Whatever Happened to Billy the Kid?* 1st edition, Sunstone Press, 1993. (p. 154)

[2] Arizona, State of. "Standard Certificate of Death of John Miller." edited by Arizona Board of Health, 1937.

[3] Fulginitti, Laura C. "Exhumation, Pioneer Home Cemetery, Prescott, Az." Office of the Maricopa County Medical Examiner, June 2, 2005 2005, p. 2.

[4] Miller, John. "Applicattion for Admission." edited by Home for Aged and Infirm Arizona Pioneers, Superior Court, 1936.

CHAPTER 10

Ambush at Stoneville, Montana

GEORGE EXELBEE, OTHERWISE known as George Axelbee, was born in the year 1860 in Indiantown, Illinois to William and Francis Exelbee. His background up to the age of about twenty is relatively unknown, but in 1879 he was known as a hard-working cowpuncher with the Hashknife outfit in the vicinity of Pecos, Texas. Young Exelbee joined a cattle drive and moved with the herd, north into New Mexico along the Goodnight-Loving Trail. The trail followed the Pecos River through New Mexico towns of Roswell, Fort Sumner, Anton Chico and north through Colorado, Wyoming and eventually ending up on Box Elder Creek, Montana.[1]

At the age of twenty, George wasn't considered young for a cowpuncher. His trail boss was a cowboy by the name of Max Narbeau, himself only twenty years of age. George was considered a tall, dark man who weighed about one hundred eighty pounds and seemed to be a solid young man. He claimed to have tuberculosis and chose outside work to improve his health. He was a hardworking cowpuncher that those who worked with him described as an average young man who minded his own business and avoided scrapes with the law.

Shortly after they reached Box Elder and the herd settled on their new range, George Exelbee quit the Hashknife outfit and became a buffalo hunter. Exelbee was camped near Hettinger, North Dakota in 1881 when Indians raided his camp and burned his buffalo hides. Destroying his camp and stealing his food, they left the place in shambles. Exelbee vowed to get even and began exacting his revenge on Indians whenever he had the occasion. Indian ponies were his main interests, and at each opportunity, he stole them and left Indians afoot. He was well-known to the outfit riders, and there were standing orders to treat him right and feed him when he rode into camp. It wasn't long before the government was after him, along with the Indians.

A short time later, he joined with a sixteen-year-old by the name of William McCarthy, who Exelbee called "Billy the Kid." Eating their dinner, they camped near a small stream in 1883 when they saw a band of eight Indians approach in the distance. Exelbee and the Kid had about eighty head of horses with them, and they expected the Indians were going to steal them. The Kid drove the horses downstream while Exelbee moved to a gully between the camp and the Indians. As they approached Exelbee's location, he opened fire with his Winchester, killing several of them. It was not the first time Exelbee killed Indians, and for the next few years, he stayed just ahead of Indians and U.S. Cavalry alike.[2]

Of course, Exelbee's Billy the Kid was not the famous Kid of New Mexico. William McCarthy came to the Dakotas and Montana country by way of Deadwood, South Dakota, where he first appeared in the company of a "freebooter" named Jack Geisler. Geisler had recently returned from Arizona when he and McCarthy allegedly killed Geisler's cousin, Ben Fiddler, a Deadwood blacksmith. Selling his ranch, Fiddler used the proceeds to outfit the trio for a Powder River buffalo hunt. Geisler and McCarthy soon returned to Deadwood reporting Fiddler dead as a result of an accident. He allegedly died when his pistol fell out of his holster and discharged a round into him. Both Geisler and McCarthy explained that they disposed of all the equipment and appropriated the funds for burial expenses. It was noted, however, that Geisler was spending a lot of money he wasn't typically known to have on gambling and drinking.[3]

Fiddler's half-sister came to Deadwood intending to cause the arrest and prosecution of Geisler and McCarthy but was unsuccessful. Unfortunately for Fiddler, the only two witnesses to his death were Geisler and McCarthy. Who could dispute their claim? About this time, McCarthy viewed his environment and his partner in an unhealthy light and eventually teamed up with George Exelbee. Together, they formed the nucleus of the Exelbee Gang joined by several grizzled types, "Bronco" or "Bad Land Charlie" Brown, Alex Grady, Hank Campbell, Henry Tuttle, and Jesse Pruden. The Exelbee Gang often referred to as the Axelby Gang, became a local legend in and around Deadwood and Spearfish, eventually attaining notoriety in Eastern newspapers.

One New York Sun writer wrote: "Mr. Axelby is said to be at the head of a trusty band as fearless and as lawless as himself. The Little Missouri and Powder River districts are the theater of his operations. An Indian is Mr. Axelby's destation. He kills him at sight if he can. He considers that Indians have no right to own ponies and he takes their ponies whenever he can. Mr. Axelby has repeatedly announced his determination he will not be taken alive. The men of the frontier say he bears a charmed life, and the hairbreath scrapes of which have made him the hero are numerous and of the wildest stamp."[4]

However, time was running out for the Axelby Gang, and fate was about to judge them in a way no courthouse could.

The gang members were riding out the bad weather of snow and temperatures of thirty degrees below zero in a saloon in

Stoneville, Montana. They were preparing to free their compatriot, Jesse Pruden, who had been arrested in Custer County, Montana, earlier for the theft of Indian ponies from the reservation. Deputy U.S. Marshall Al Raymond originally planned to return Pruden to Deadwood for trial. Returning to Spearfish, South Dakota, he sent another deputy, Joe Ryan, after Pruden. Sheriff Johnson of Custer County turned Pruden over to Ryan and furnished two deputies to ride with him back to Deadwood. The sheriff then telegraphed the authorities in Deadwood that most likely, the Axelby Gang would attempt to rescue Pruden, and the sheriff requested a posse from Deadwood meet the Ryan group.

U.S. Marshall Fred Willard's office was in Spearfish, and although his primary responsibility was to arrest deserters from nearby Fort Meade, he, Lawrence County Deputy Sheriff Jack O'Hara, and M.C. Alderbeau departed Deadwood to meet Ryan and his prisoner. At nearly the same time, a posse consisting of Deputy U.S. Marshall Cap Willard, John Duffy and Frank Jackson arrived in Spearfish only to learn the other posse had already left and the Deadwood group hurried to overtake them. Alderbeau was unable to keep up with the Spearfish posse and was left behind by Fred Willard. When Willard's group arrived in Stoneville on February 14, 1884, they went to the home of Lou Stone and learned George Exelbee and six outlaws were in the saloon only two hundred yards up the road.

The Axelby Gang was unaware that two posses were converging on their location. When the gang exited the saloon, they mounted their horses and leading a spare horse and a packhorse, prepared to leave Stoneville. Attempting to stop the band from going, Fred Willard and Deputy O'Hara ran out of the Stone house and opened fire. There was one member, however, who was late in leaving. Cap Willard and Alderbeau heard the gunshots and hurried into town. Dismounting quickly, he fired on the gang members. The first two to go down were bystanders named William Cunningham and Jack Harris, though they were initially believed to be part of the gang. Both men died of their wounds. Their deaths were undoubtedly a case of being in the wrong place at the wrong time.

Jack Campbell was a victim of a grazing shot in the head. He was killed the following day by the posse after he tried to escape the area. Henry Tuttle was shot in the left elbow, badly breaking his arm. Tuttle received treatment, and members of the posse transported him to Spearfish where a vigilante committee hauled him out of the hospital one night and lynched him. Willard's group shot Exelbee's horse from beneath him, and he received a severe bullet wound in the thigh. The one gang member who was late in leaving was the Kid. He ran out of the saloon and engaged the posse men from a corral post. Using his Winchester, he caught them in a crossfire and killed O'Hara. His return fire allowed the remaining outlaws to escape Stoneville. Apparently, "Bronco" Charlie Brown, Alex Grady and the Kid did not receive severe wounds.[5]

Unfortunately, the shootout at Stoneville did not end the escapades of George Exelbee and William McCarthy. Both men continued their predation of Indian ponies, but eventually, the duo disappeared. In 1889, another well-known rustler of the Pecos River region in New Mexico, Martin Mrose, expressed that he had seen both Exelbee and McCarthy.

A.P. "Ott" Black related in his book, *The End of the Long Horn Trail*: "I worked with Martin Marose (Mrose) in 1889, and he told me that Axelby (Exelbee) and "The Kid" rode into Clayton Wells, New Mexico, a short time afterward (Stoneville shootout). They were bound for the Mexican border. Clayton Wells was nothing much more than a cattle ranch headquarters at the time—only one adobe house, and a couple

CHAPTER 10: AMBUSH AT STONEVILLE, MONTANA | 165

of horse-powered wells. It was the headquarters of the VVN ranch, set out on a forty square mile flat of sand and Chinnery and stretched out as far as the eye could see. Axelby and the kid were heading for Mexico and had swum the Pecos about forty miles west of the Wells. Marose (Mrose) said they rode in and spread eight thousand dollars in greenbacks all over the inside of the house and made that adobe shack as hot as a furnace. As soon as the money dried, they rode off to the south."[6]

Martin Mrose was himself a colorful character in the Pecos River Basin, having stolen upwards of twenty thousand cattle. After killing a man near Seven Rivers, New Mexico, Mrose fled to Mexico. His wife, Helen Beulah Mrose, boarded a train to El Paso and immediately began working to keep her husband, Martin, from the hangman's noose. In fighting her husband's extradition, she retained the services of a young attorney recently paroled out of Huntsville Prison in Texas, where he studied law and passed the bar exam. His name was John Wesley Hardin. Martin Mrose was his first case. But Hardin was attracted to Helen's charms and soon realized it was to his advantage that Martin Mrose stayed in Mexico. Learning that people routinely saw his wife in the company of Hardin, Mrose allowed himself to be lured across the border to see Helen. Deputy U.S. Marshall Frank McMahan and another shooter waited for Mrose and ambushed him. When they buried Mrose the next day, his death certificate lists his last illness as *"gunshot wound"* and the length of his illness as lasting *"one minute."*[7]

So, one might ask, "What does George Exelbee have to do with John Miller?" The story may be a reach, but some coincidental factors are tying them together. Martin Mrose brings nothing to the story except that I thought it was humorous. That aside, it is possible that John Miller was George Exelbee.

Figure 19. John Miller wearing a pistol with a belt and leather chaps. Reprinted with permission from Anita Liston, daughter and heir to the original owner, Jewel Crocket Lambson. © Anita Liston.

Figure 20. John Miller wearing leather chaps. Reprinted with permission from Anita Liston, daughter and heir to the original owner, Jewel Crocket Lambson. © Anita Liston.

Let's look at some of the similarities. John Miller told Frank Creasy that he was involved in a bank robbery in Montana where several members of his gang were killed. He said he and one other outlaw got away with eight thousand dollars divided into two sums, four thousand dollars each. He said he bought his pardon with four thousand dollars. George Exelbee was involved in a shootout with a posse in Stoneville, Montana in 1884 where lawmen killed several members of his gang. Several sources reflected that only he and his compatriot survived.

Martin Mrose reported seeing the Kid and Exelbee riding hard for Mexico. They crossed the Pecos River and stopped at an adobe ranch house at Clayton Wells. After plastering the walls with eight thousand dollars in currency, they built a hot fire to dry it out.

John and Isadora Miller both reported in the U.S. Censuses of 1900 and 1910 that they married in 1886. We learned from genealogy records that Isadora Miller was probably Isadora Gurule from Anton Chico, New Mexico. Since George Exelbee and the Kid were running from the law and were in the vicinity of Anton Chico in 1885-1886, it's possible George found himself enamored with a young Mexican woman and returned to her. Since he was about the same age as the real Billy the Kid, she may have even believed at first, he was the outlaw shot by Pat Garrett. Changing his name was nothing unusual during this time. Most outlaws changed their names on occasion to fit their needs. We initially questioned the origin of the team of horses, a wagon and milk cows the Millers traveled with to Western New Mexico. Four thousand dollars pays for a lot of supplies and livestock. What's more, Exelbee worked in Eastern New Mexico on the way to Montana during the time of Billy the Kid and would have accumulated some information about him. If he was John Miller, this information would have provided him

CHAPTER 10: AMBUSH AT STONEVILLE, MONTANA | 169

Figure 21. George Exelbee about age 24 years. Notice belt buckle and leather chaps. Unknown photographer, reprinted with permission from Doug Engebretson. © Doug Engebretson.

with a foundation for a claim of identity.

Another curious point, both Miller and Exelbee received bullet wounds to the upper right thigh. Miller claimed it was from a shootout with a posse, but never claimed he received the wound during the Battle of Lincoln. Exelbee's wound did in fact result from a shootout with a posse.

Creasy said John always had access to money. Could this $8000 have been the cash to which he referred? Creasy also noted that a young man by the name of Jesus Cacouse frequented the Miller place. Examining U.S. Census records of Guadalupe County, Texas from 1880 to 1910, I located several members of the Cacouse family. Could it be that the Kid from Montana made it to that area and after working for the Cacouse family, changed his name? It is possible that Miller's occasional youthful visitor, Jesus Cacouse was William McCarthy, the Montana Billy the Kid.

Since everyone seems to like photo comparisons, look at the photos of John Miller and George Exelbee. Each is wearing leather chaps, and the gun belt buckles are the same. They even exhibit the same gun-toting slant. Both John and George display the same configuration with their gun hands, and both wear their hats at the same angle. Distinguishing between the two is difficult because of their ages and the poor quality of the photographs, but there is some resemblance. While Miller seems shorter than Exelbee, his shoulder configuration is similar, and his facial features compare reasonably to those of Exelbee, even after aging. The similarities between timing and photographic nuances are interesting, but not conclusive.

Of course, there are problems with this entire assessment because it is all based on pure conjecture. If George Exelbee were born in 1860, then by 1910 his age would be only 50 years old. However, in Helen Airy's book, she identified John Miller's photo as having been taken when he was about fifty years old. A hard life could account for some of the aging, but it is difficult to conclude they are positively photos of the same individual. As for the chaps, during that period, leather chaps were not that unusual, and I am reasonably sure the similar gun belt buckles were probably not unique. However, Miller is wearing what appears to be the same leather chaps in all the photos taken of him.

George Exelbee is well dressed in his picture and seems to present himself as a prosperous cowboy. It's hard to believe that if John Miller was George Exelbee, his features and style of dress deteriorated to the extent displayed in his photographs. Understandably, poverty, and illness over time have a way of diminishing the spark of life in a person. If Exelbee was Miller, thirty years of a harsh existence had a dramatic effect on Miller's appearance.

There was one other person who might have been John Miller of Ramah, New Mexico. His name was also John Miller. He was a gambler residing in Georgetown, Grant County, New Mexico, and he listed his marital status as married. His marital status suggests that if he was our John Miller from Ramah, he was married to someone other than Isadora. He listed the birthplace of both his mother and father as Missouri.

While I was unable to find any background that indicated he knew anything about ranching or that he was even aware of the history of Billy the Kid, the information contained in the U.S. Census of 1880 was intriguing and could be fodder for more re-search. His birth date was about 1850, and place of birth was listed as Texas. While there were matching details between his demo-graphic information with some of John Miller of Ramah, there is a record of his death in 1904. His compatriots buried him in the Memory Lane Cemetery, Silver

City, New Mexico, so he was probably not the John Miller of Ramah.

There may be other John Millers, and a diligent researcher might find more reflective records. The difficulty with someone who wants to hide is that they create many false trails by providing inaccurate information. John and Isadora were masters in that creativity when it came to providing information to the census taker. With that said, the older they became, the more information they provided by error or as a result of conscience. We can only deduce their true identities based on little clues they left with us. In the end, there is nothing conclusive to prove who they were; they were pioneers and led exciting lives.

Regardless, pioneer accounts while interesting, had only anecdotal relevance to the Millers' chronicle. Anatomical, anthropological, historical, and medical evidence not only refute many tales told about John Miller; I believe they discredit any claim that he was Billy the Kid. However, I recognize I am only the investigator. I have presented evidence in support of a conclusion. But I am not the jury, and I can leave the decision to the reader. The final question to be asked is, "In comparing the detailed physical attributes of Billy the Kid to those of John Miller, can one conclude that both men were the same person?"

---

[1] Black, A.P. (Ott). *The End of the Long Horn Trail.* The Selfridge Journal, 1936.

[2] Ibid. (pp.10-17)

[3] McClintock, John S. *Pioneer Days in the Black Hills: By One of the Early Day Pioneers.* edited by Edward L. Senn, University of Oklahoma Press, 1939. (pp. 196-197)

⁴ Engebretson, Doug. *The George Axelby Gang and the Stoneville Battle.* Self, Unknown. (p.8-21)

⁵ ---. *Empty Saddles, Forgotten Names: Outlaws of the Black Hills and Wyoming.* North Plains Press, 1982. (pp. 145-153)

⁶ Black, A.P. (Ott). *The End of the Long Horn Trail.* The Selfridge Journal, 1936. (p. 17)

⁷ McCown, Dennis. *The Goddess of War.* Sunstone Press, 2013. (p. 166)

CHAPTER 11

The Next Man in Line

WILLIAM BONNEY, ALIAS Billy the Kid, whether he died, or he lived beyond July 14, 1881, is now for sure, dead. Somewhere, they buried the truth of his death with him, and all we are left to consider are anecdotal stories and remaining clues he left behind. Quite often distorted, anecdotal accounts are frequently inaccurate; not necessarily false but sometimes flawed by age and exaggerated recollection. The imperfections and discrepancies will forever remain. No answers will be forthcoming; only further debate and more questions. Someone is wrong about the real death of William Bonney, but conversely, someone is right. We can only surmise through inference, that the Kid might or might not have survived that night. However, there can only be one William Bonney, alias Billy the Kid. Either he was killed and planted in the ground, or he lived on to a ripe old age. The question now is, if he lived, who did he become?

We may never know which is correct; probably an unprovable conundrum. I coined a phrase while working on my dissertation, "There is the truth, and there is history. The truth may be unattainable; history is what we believe. Only facts separate the two." There is proof, however, that John Miller cannot legitimately claim the identity of William H. Bonney.

John Miller was not the only person to claim the identity of Billy the Kid. Over the years there have been several, most failing to meet the thresholds of proof. Falling into obscurity, they passed into history as well.

There was, however, one other man who surfaced in the late 1940s who also claimed to be Billy the Kid. He engendered a significant following, and today many believe he was the true William H. Bonney of legend. He appeared before Governor Thomas Mabry on November 29, 1950, to ask for a pardon in the name of William Bonney but the results were disastrous for him. He was mocked by the Governor and his visitors alike who were present to question him about his past. Governor Mabry refused to pardon the man saying, "I am taking no action, now or ever, on this application for a pardon for Billy, the Kid because I do not believe this man is Billy the Kid."[1]

Ultimately, the man returned to his residence in Hico, Texas, and while mailing a package on December 27, 1950, his heart stopped. He died on the street with one arm draped over the bumper of a car parked next to the curb. His name was Oliver P. Roberts, alias "Brushy Bill" Roberts.

---

[1] Sonnichsen, C. L. and William Vincent Morrison. *Alias Billy the Kid "... I Want to Die a Free Man ...".* University of New Mexico Press, 1955.

EPILOGUE

IN MY NEXT BOOK, I conduct an extensive analysis of the claim by Oliver P. "Brushy Bill" Roberts, that he was Billy the Kid. Utilizing similar methods as those used to evaluate claims by John Miller and others, I will unmask "Brushy Bill" Roberts and uncover his legacy. Maybe "Brushy Bill" was Billy the Kid and maybe he wasn't. Psycholinguistics and content analysis will cut through the inuendo and conjecture to the meat of evidence that either proves or disproves his claim.

"Brushy Bill" also had a strong ally. His name was William V. Morrison and after his passing, he left hundreds of documents not fully examined until only recently. A treasure trove of evidence tells the real story, not only about Morrison and "Brushy Bill" but Billy the Kid as well. Using science, technology and investigative technique, I break down the connections and conflicts that lead to new revelations. Once again, facts will unmask the legend.

Watch for my book about "Brushy Bill" Roberts in the Spring of 2020. If you like historical crime mysteries, this book will not disappoint you.

In the meantime, if you like FREE reports and "How to . . ." articles about the technologies I use, visit my publisher's website at www.WesternLegendsResearch.com and pickup your FREE copies.

Thanks,
Dale Tunnell

APPENDICES

APPENDIX I – LETTER FRAGMENT 1879

SCALE	Score	SD from Mean
Death Anxiety	1.277	1.916
Mutilation Anxiety	0.792	0.785
Separation Anxiety	0.408	0.000
Guilt Anxiety	0.865	1.133
Shame Anxiety	0.601	0.000
Diffuse Anxiety	0.401	0.000
Total Anxiety	1.796	0.452
Hostility Out - Overt	0.755	0.000
Hostility Out - Covert	0.746	0.166
Total Hostility Out	1.136	0.333
Hostility Inward	0.688	0.000
Ambivalent Hostility	0.653	0.000
Social Alienation-Personal Disorganization	-2.220	0.248
Cognitive Impairment	0.684	-3.178
Hope	0.299	-0.428
Hopelessness	0.599	-0.972
Self-Accusation	1.139	0.187
Psychomotor Retardation	0.305	0.000
Somatic Concerns	0.612	0.000
Death and Mutilation Depression	1.351	0.648
Separation Depression	0.408	0.000
Hostility Directed Outward	1.136	0.136
Total Depression	6.077	0.319
Health	0.000	0.000
Sickness	1.072	3.552
Health/Sickness	-1.072	-4.306
Human Relations	-0.134	-1.326
Support	2.413	0.579
Deterrents	-1.340	-3.853
Achievement Strivings	1.072	-0.032
Dependency Strivings	1.340	1.906

APPENDIX I (CONT.) – LETTER FRAGMENT 1879

SCALE	Score	SD from Mean
Dependency Strivings	1.340	1.906
Frustrated Dependency	0.536	2.368
Narcissism	0.536	0.000
Quality of Life	-1.925	0.537

APPENDIX II – LETTER TO FRIEND WILSON
MARCH 20, 1879

SCALE	Score	SD from Mean
Death Anxiety	0.821	0.000
Mutilation Anxiety	0.646	0.000
Separation Anxiety	0.570	0.000
Guilt Anxiety	0.773	0.000
Shame Anxiety	1.905	2.605
Diffuse Anxiety	0.700	0.000
Total Anxiety	1.992	0.731
Hostility Out - Overt	0.886	0.000
Hostility Out - Covert	0.726	0.121
Total Hostility Out	1.116	0.292
Hostility Inward	0.878	0.000
Ambivalent Hostility	0.724	0.000
Social Alienation-Personal Disorganization	-0.030	0.000
Cognitive Impairment	0.793	-0.036
Hope	0.581	-0.154
Hopelessness	0.417	0.000
Self-Accusation	2.101	1.846
Psychomotor Retardation	0.358	0.000
Somatic Concerns	0.883	0.000
Death and Mutilation Depression	0.821	0.000

APPENDIX II (CONT.) – LETTER TO FRIEND WILSON
MARCH 20, 1879

SCALE	Score	SD from Mean
Separation Depression	0.570	0.000
Hostility Directed Outward	1.116	0.100
Total Depression	6.514	0.553
Health	0.000	0.000
Sickness	0.000	0.000
Health/Sickness	0.000	0.000
Human Relations	1.031	0.112
Support	0.000	0.000
Deterrents	-1.031	-3.279
Achievement Strivings	-1.031	-1.830
Dependency Strivings	0.000	0.000
Frustrated Dependency	0.000	0.000
Narcissism	1.031	0.000
Quality of Life	-4.872	-0.449

APPENDIX III – LETTER TO LEW WALLACE
MARCH 20, 1879

SCALE	Score	SD from Mean
Death Anxiety	1.545	2.441
Mutilation Anxiety	0.455	0.000
Separation Anxiety	0.776	1.036
Guilt Anxiety	1.056	1.522
Shame Anxiety	0.620	0.000
Diffuse Anxiety	1.674	2.879
Total Anxiety	2.763	1.832
Hostility Out - Overt	0.942	0.671
Hostility Out - Covert	0.705	0.076

APPENDIX III (CONT.) – LETTER TO LEW WALLACE
MARCH 20, 1879

SCALE	Score	SD from Mean
Ambivalent Hostility	0.881	0.700
Social Alienation-Personal Disorganization	-2.283	0.225
Cognitive Impairment	-0.546	-2.886
Hope	0.088	-0.633
Hopelessness	0.693	-0.667
Self-Accusation	1.557	0.909
Psychomotor Retardation	0.351	0.010
Somatic Concerns	0.848	5.083
Death and Mutilation Depression	1.349	0.644
Separation Depression	0.776	-0.118
Hostility Directed Outward	1.158	0.176
Total Depression	7.867	1.276
Health	0.302	-0.376
Sickness	1.813	6.636
Health/Sickness	-1.511	-5.401
Human Relations	-1.057	-2.466
Support	1.813	-0.028
Deterrents	-1.208	-3.608
Achievement Strivings	0.604	-4.32
Dependency Strivings	0.604	0.153
Frustrated Dependency	0.000	0.000
Narcissism	0.000	0.000
Quality of Life	-3.925	-0.132

APPENDIX IV – LETTER TO LEW WALLACE, DECEMBER 12, 1880

SCALE	Score	SD from Mean
Death Anxiety	1.059	1.489
Mutilation Anxiety	0.752	0.712
Separation Anxiety	0.957	1.427
Guilt Anxiety	0.367	0.000
Shame Anxiety	0.520	0.000
Diffuse Anxiety	0.320	0.000
Total Anxiety	2.090	0.871
Hostility Out - Overt	0.720	0.000
Hostility Out - Covert	0.674	0.008
Total Hostility Out	1.064	0.187
Hostility Inward	1.128	1.509
Ambivalent Hostility	0.634	0.000
Social Alienation-Personal Disorganization	-0.915	0.731
Cognitive Impairment	0.737	-0.156
Hope	0.309	-0.419
Hopelessness	0.623	-0.895
Self-Accusation	1.462	0.745
Psychomotor Retardation	0.291	0.000
Somatic Concerns	0.539	0.000
Death and Mutilation Depression	1.211	0.433
Separation Depression	0.957	0.136
Hostility Directed Outward	1.064	0.006
Total Depression	6.830	0.722
Health	1.324	2.628
Sickness	0.588	1.534
Health/Sickness	0.735	0.213
Human Relations	-0.074	-1.251
Support	2.647	0.815

APPENDIX IV (CONT.) – LETTER TO LEW WALLACE, DECEMBER 12, 1880

SCALE	Score	SD from Mean
Deterrents	-0.882	-3.004
Achievement Strivings	1.765	0.560
Dependency Strivings	0.147	-0.936
Frustrated Dependency	0.147	0.206
Narcissism	0.294	0.000
Quality of Life	-5.598	-0.692

APPENDIX V – LETTER TO LEW WALLACE, MARCH 4, 1881

SCALE	Score	SD from Mean
Death Anxiety	0.587	0.000
Mutilation Anxiety	0.499	0.000
Separation Anxiety	0.881	1.262
Guilt Anxiety	0.542	0.000
Shame Anxiety	0.685	0.000
Diffuse Anxiety	0.485	0.000
Total Anxiety	1.546	0.094
Hostility Out - Overt	0.792	0.000
Hostility Out - Covert	0.515	0.000
Total Hostility Out	0.905	0.000
Hostility Inward	1.051	1.287
Ambivalent Hostility	0.826	0.571
Social Alienation-Personal Disorganization	-3.311	-0.156
Cognitive Impairment	-1.111	-4.088
Hope	0.997	0.250
Hopelessness	0.697	-0.653
Self-Accusation	1.334	0.524
Psychomotor Retardation	0.320	0.000

APPENDIX V (CONT.) – LETTER TO LEW WALLACE, MARCH 4, 1881

SCALE	Score	SD from Mean
Somatic Concerns	0.687	0.000
Death and Mutilation Depression	0.651	0.000
Separation Depression	0.881	0.029
Hostility Directed Outward	0.905	0.000
Total Depression	6.016	0.287
Health	0.862	1.271
Sickness	0.431	0.879
Health/Sickness	0.431	-0.547
Human Relations	0.000	0.000
Support	1.293	-0.552
Deterrents	-0.862	-2.967
Achievement Strivings	0.431	-0.580
Dependency Strivings	0.431	-0.259
Frustrated Dependency	0.000	0.000
Narcissism	0.000	0.000
Quality of Life	-1.023	0.839

APPENDIX VI

Psychiatric Content Analysis and Diagnosis[1]

Reprint permission granted by Robert Bechtel, Ph.D., developer and owner of GB Software, LLC.

Theoretical Background and Development

Introduction

The Gottschalk-Gleser Content Analysis Method for measuring the magnitude of various psychobiological states and traits from the content analysis of verbal behavior has been successfully applied to many different neuropsychiatric dimensions. Extensive empirical research has established the validity and reliability of scales measuring a variety of emotional and psychobiological states including anxiety (including death, mutilation, separation, guilt, shame, and diffuse anxiety subscales), hostility outward (including overt hostility, covert hostility, and total hostility outward subscales), hostility inward, ambivalent hostility (hostility originating externally and directed towards the self), social alienation-personal disorganization, cognitive impairment, hope, depression (including seven subscales), human relations, achievement strivings, dependency, strivings, and health/ sickness.[2]

While the utility of these scales has been demonstrated repeatedly through decades of research, widespread everyday use of content analysis of verbal behavior for research and clinical practice has been hampered by the relatively high training and performance requirements associated with the manual application of the technique. For example, Gottschalk and Gleser recommend an inter-coder reliability coefficient of 0.80 or better with the scoring of qualified experts in the use of these content analysis scales. To achieve this level of familiarity and skill in coding these scales requires some practice with previously published and unpublished examples of scoring these content analysis scales and continual monitoring of trained scorers. Manual scoring is also not a particularly quick process, requiring trained not only content judgments but also extensive post-processing of scores to prepare scale-based summaries and analyses.

Brief Descriptions of the Content Analysis Scales

The full definition of each of the scales available for computerized scoring is included later in this appendix. This section provides a narrative description of the various scales. Reliability and validity studies for each of these scales have been published in the literature and references are available either from GB Software or from our web page.

Anxiety Scale

The type of anxiety that this scale measures is what could be termed "free" anxiety in contrast to "bound" anxiety, which manifests itself in psychobiological mechanisms of conversion and hypochondriacal symptoms, in compulsions, in doing and undoing, in withdrawal from human relationships, and so forth. Some aspects of bound anxiety are registered by this scale, mainly using displacement and denial. This type of bound anxiety is relatively accessible to consciousness, usually in defensive form and is capable, along with grossly conscious "free" anxiety feelings, of activating the autonomic nervous system and central nervous system signs of arousal.

Based on clinical observation, the Anxiety Scale is classified into six subtypes: death, mutilation, separation, guilt, shame, and diffuse or non-specific anxiety. The identity of content items dealing directly with death and destruction is a means to assess fear of death. Mutilation anxiety is synonymous with "castration" anxiety, and we derive the descriptive details in the scale of this subtype of stress as well as the concept of separation anxiety from clinical psychoanalytic psychology. We also investigate what significant issues evolve from references in the speech included under this heading. The expressive things differentiating shame from guilt anxiety distinguish shame through verbal references to ridicule, inadequacy, embarrassment, humiliation, exposure of shortcomings or details of a person's private life and identify guilt through verbal references to adverse criticism, abuse, condemnation, or moral disapproval, primarily based on internalized attitudes or values. Diffuse or non-specific anxiety is the category of stress in the scale where it is impossible to distinguish the type of anxiety-fear in the speech sample.

Hostility Scales

The Hostility Scales are designed to measure three types of the hostility of a transient, rather than sustained affect. The hostility scores derived from several verbal samples obtained from the same individual will provide a trait-like measure.

The Hostility Directed Outward Scale measures the intensity of adversely critical, angry, assaultive, asocial impulses and drives towards objects outside oneself.

The Hostility Directed Inward Scale measures degrees of self-hate and self-criticisms and, to some extent, feelings of anxious depression and masochism.

The Ambivalent Hostility Scale, though derived from verbal communications suggesting destructive and critical thoughts or actions of others to the self, also measures not only some aspects of hostility directed inward, but at the same time, some features of hatred directed outwards.

All three hostility scales assign higher weights to scorable verbal statements communicating hostility that, by inference, is more likely to be strongly experienced by the speaker; whereas, completely repressed hostility is not scored.

Social Alienation-Personal Disorganization Scale

This scale was initially designed to measure the relative degree of personal disorganization, social alienation, and isolation of schizophrenic patients. The common denominators of the schizophrenic syndrome are considered to be disturbances in the coherence and logicality of thinking processes and disorders in human relationships, especially in the form of withdrawal, avoidance, and antagonism. Another principal characteristic of this concept of the schizophrenic syndrome is that it is a phenomenon quantitatively describabable, that is, there are relative degrees of severity of schizophrenia and, in some schizophrenic individuals, severity can fluctuate considerably from day-to-day.

This concept of the schizophrenic syndrome, in fact, holds that these principals, and characteristic features of schizophrenia—social alienation and personal disorganization—are present to a varying extent in non-schizophrenic individuals but not in such a continuous and extreme fashion as in schizophrenia.

Cognitive and Intellectual Impairment Scale

The Cognitive and Intellectual Impairment Scale is designed to measure transient and reversible changes in cognitive and intellectual functions as well as permanent and irreversible changes, all due principally to brain dysfunction and minimally to temporary emotional changes in the individual.

Hope Scale

The Hope Scale is designed to measure the intensity of the optimism that a favorable outcome is likely to occur, not only in one's personal earthly activities but also to cosmic phenomena and even in spiritual or imaginary events. The desirable outcome is intended to denote one which might lead to human survival, the preservation or enhancement of health, the welfare or constructive achievement of the self, or any part of humankind.

Depression Scale

This Depression Scale, derived from verbal samples, provides measurement dimensions compatible with the concept that there are several potentially relevant subcategories of the construct of depression, which have significant statistical relationships with different underlying pathogenic processes. Thus, in addition to providing a total score, it has a broad range of phenomenological subscales. These are:

- Hopelessness
- Self-Accusation
- Psychomotor Retardation
- Somatic Concerns
- Death and Mutilation Depression
- Separation Depression
- Hostility Outward

Human Relations Scale

This scale provides a quantitative estimate of an individual's degree of interest in and his capacity for constructive, mutually productive, or satisfying human relationships. The impetus for developing this scale stemmed from the clinical impression that the relative magnitude of such ability or need has often seemed to be an essential factor in how a patient responds to brief psychotherapy. How successfully a person is advancing in a career involving mutual collaboration and dependence on other people, or even how successfully one learns at school from other people are also essential factors.

Achievement Strivings Scale

The purpose of this scale is to provide a means to assess both the transient swings and normal levels of motivation toward achievement and also the relative magnitude of reactions of frustration in this drive. We have not found content categories which can cover achievement strivings and accomplishments relevant to all possible fields of endeavor, since vocational and avocational strivings may be differentially pertinent, and since one person's vocation may be another person's pastime. It may be necessary to specify the achievement goals of the subjects studied to assess the meaning of any findings.

Dependency Strivings Scale

The purpose of this scale is to provide a means to assess both the transient swings and normal levels of motivation toward dependency and the relative magnitude of reactions of frustration in this drive.

Health-Sickness Scale

This scale distinguishes references to good and bad health, and reports each separately, together with a combined measure of total referrals to health issues.

Narcissistic Scale

The Narcissistic Scale was devised from a synthesis of descriptions from the scientific literature on narcissistic patients and healthy narcissistic individuals. It provides an objective measure of the relative magnitude of narcissism. The characteristic captured in the Narcissistic Scale appears to be the degree to which a person feels entitlement versus a sense of responsibility for his or her accomplishments and failures.

Healthy narcissism consists of the recognition that one's attributes and the attributes of others are, in no small degree, the products of choices that a person makes in life and not due to the presence or absence of some mysterious fate, birthright, or entitlement. The Narcissistic Scale should be considered experimental: no norms have been established, and research is continuing.

Quality of Life Scale

This Scale is a composite of several other scales and attempts to represent a measure of the overall quality (positive or negative) of the subject's life, as revealed in the sample.

Rationale

A clinician has several options in obtaining objective and valid clinical evaluations. For example, precision and accuracy may be avoided, and impressionistic reactions and "gut feelings" can be relied on; some clinicians feel they can do competent clinical work with this approach. Or a clinician can spend considerable time and care in the diagnostic and therapeutic evaluation of children and adults to assess accurately and precisely the magnitude of diverse psychopathological processes within patients at different times.

Another approach is to use various observer psychiatric rating scales, such as the Brief Psychiatric Rating Scale, the Hamilton Anxiety or Depression Rating Scales or various self-report measures, such as different adjective checklists. Although many research projects use these measures, their use carries with them a false sense of security since quite often no inter-rater reliability tests are done with the rating scales, the assumption being that anybody can follow the instructions for rating and no measurement errors are likely to occur. With rating scales, however, raters vary widely on how much of the range of ratings they use with the same subjects, and some evaluators characteristically select the lower range of the scores; whereas others habitually chose the higher range of the scores. With self-report measures, though the self-rating comes directly from the individual's speech, the assumption is that self-raters are all, in equivalent contact with themselves and are not likely to falsify, consciously or unconsciously, their self-evaluations.

These kinds of measurement errors in observer rating scales

and self-report scales, usually disregarded by researchers and clinicians, are minimized in the measurement method of content analysis of verbal behavior. For the subjects being rated are generally not aware of what speech content or form is being analyzed and have difficulty covering up, even if they have some notions about such matters. Furthermore, the unstructured approach customarily used to elicit speech avoids the questionnaire or "prosecuting attorney" method and allows the subject to elaborate and use free-will to the extent desired by the self on a choice of topics to verbalize. Emotions, self-reflections, doubts, and defensive maneuvers all contribute to the content analysis scores eventually calculated. The content analysis approach to the measurement of psychological dimensions include the strengths of both the self-report approach and the observer rating scale approach and minimizes the weaknesses of both in terms of measurement errors.

Development of the Scales

The development of an objective and reliable method of measuring the magnitude of various psychological dimensions from natural language was motivated by the recognition that diagnosticians and therapists use speech as a significant source of information. In doing so, they assess how and what their client says in an impressionistic manner that allows for a relatively high likelihood of distortion and error from potentially incorrect empathic responses and inferences during the process of evaluating the subject's talk. How to minimize such error variance and how to maximize the uniformity and consistency of the inferential evaluations concerning the speaker's subjective experience and the relative magnitude of these psychological states and conflicts became a compelling aim.

In the process of probing the emotional reactions of subjects or patients, an effort was made to minimize reactions of guarding or covering. Hence the instructions to elicit speech from the issue were purposely relatively ambiguous and non-structured. Speakers were asked to tell about personal or dramatic life experiences. From such standardized guidelines, we found it possible to explore and investigate demographic and personality traits to compare individuals in a standard context while holding relatively constant the influence of such variables as the instructions for eliciting speech, the nature, and character of the interviewer, the setting, and the situation. Examiners subsequently investigated the effects of varying these non-interviewee variables one by one, after developing reliable and valid content analysis scales.

The development of the Gottschalk-Gleser method of content analysis has involved a long series of steps.

1. It has required that the psychological dimensions to be measured (for example, anxiety, hostility outward, hostility inward, cognitive and intellectual impairment, social alienation-personal disorganization, depression, and hope) be precisely defined;
2. that the lexical cues be carefully pinpointed by which a receiver of any verbal messages infer the occurrence of any of these psychological states;
3. the linguistic, principally syntactic, cues conveying intensity (for example, the word "very" in the proper context) be specified.
4. Next, we assigned differential weights to these semantic and linguistic cues conveying the magnitude of a subjective experience whenever appropriate.
5. Furthermore, we had to arrive at a systematic means for correcting for the number of words spoken per unit of time so that one individual could be compared to himself on different occasions or to others with regards to the

magnitude of any particular psychological state.

6. A series of weighted thematic categories had to be specified for every psychological dimension to be measured and;

7. research technicians were trained to score these typescripts of human speech according to any one scale an at inter-scorer reliability of 0.80 or above.

8. Moreover, a set of construct-validation studies had to be carried out to recheck specifically what each content analysis scale measured, and these validation studies have included the use of four kinds of criterion measures: psychological, physiological, pharmacological, and biochemical.

9. Based on these construct-validation studies, we made changes in the content categories and their assigned weights of each specific scale, in the direction of maximizing the correlations between the content analysis scores with these various independent criterion measures.

The theoretical framework from which this measurement approach we developed has been an eclectic one and has included behavioral and conditioning theory, psychoanalytic clinic theory, and linguistic theory. Also, the position that they all have biologic roots profoundly influenced the formulation of these psychological states.

The content analysis technician applying this procedure to typescripts of tape-recorded speech has not had to worry about approaching the work of the content analysis following one theoretical orientation or another. Instead, the technician follows a strictly empirical approach, scoring the occurrence of any content or themes in each grammatical clause of speech according to a set of various, well-delineated language categories making up each of the separate verbal behavior scales. Two manuals (Gottschalk, Winget, Gleser, 1969; Gottschalk, 1982) and a book are available as well as journal articles (Gottschalk, 1975; Gottschalk and Hoigaard-Martin, 1986) which indicate what verbal categories we should examine and how much the occurrence of each one is to be weighted. Following initial coding of content in this way, the content analysis technician, then, follows prescribed mathematical calculations leading up to the final score for the magnitude of any one psychological dimension or another.

Many individuals, mostly researchers, have achieved an acceptable level of proficiency coding the content and form analysis of verbal behavior, correctly, scoring content analysis scales based on the Gottschalk-Gleser content analysis method, and they have published excellent work involving them. Some investigators or clinicians, however, have not wanted to take the time or acquire the expertise to use these content analysis scales reliably.

Digest of Known Uses

The Gottschalk-Gleser content analysis method provides a means of making many kinds of measurements in psychology and neuropsychiatry, including the frequency of psychological changes, making initial diagnostic formulations, offering suggestions for further evaluations (if necessary), and serving as guidelines for possible therapeutic interventions. It has been used in psychotherapy research to measure changes occurring in adults and children during the process of therapy, to predict a psychotherapeutic outcome, to evaluate the psychotherapeutic outcome, to assess the importance of defense mechanisms (such as displacement and denial) in different diagnostic groups of clients, and even to teach psychodynamic psychotherapy.

It has been used to measure the relative severity of many mental and neuropsychiatric disorders, such as anxiety disorders, schizophrenia, depression, and dementia in aging and with alcohol abuse, and cognitive impairment associated with other drugs, such as, marijuana and the benzodiazepines It has been used in and recommended for psychosomatic research. It has been used to study the effects of partial and total body irradiation and sensory overload. It has proven to be very useful in neuropsychopharmacology studies, such as in the testing of new antianxiety drugs, the effects of tranquilizers, antidepressants, analgesics, and in studying the relationship of the pharmacokinetics of psychoactive medications, and clinical response. It has been widely used to assess the emotional status of medically ill patients, for example, in diabetes mellitus, with bruxism, with mastectomy for breast cancer and with cholecystectomy, and with attention-deficit-hyperactive children.

More recently it has been used to assess the quality of life as well as the relationship of cerebral glucose metabolic rates (as determined by positron emission tomography) and emotions occurring during dreams or silent wakeful mentation or while feeling hopeful or hopeless. Two other thought-provoking applications of this content analysis method involved reviewing and demonstrating its cross-cultural validity and using it to assess the relative degree of cognitive impairment manifested by presidential candidates during their campaign debates.

---

[1] Gottschalk, Louis A. and Robert J. Bechtel. "Pcad 3: Psychiatric Content Analysis and Diagnosis." 2016.

[2] Gottschalk, Louis A. *Content Analysis of Verbal Behavior: New Findings and Clinical Applications.* Lawrence Erlbaum Associates, Inc., 1995.

ACKNOWLEDGEMENTS

MORE THAN ANYONE, I wish to thank my wife Deborah for all her input and hours of proofreading my manuscripts. Without her continuous encouragement, I would never have completed this book. Many thanks also to Rich Lombardo for his continued support and reassurance. I also wish to thank Steve Sederwall for all his investigative input and those many years of discussion regarding Billy the Kid and John Miller. And to Dr. Laura Fulginitti whose report and technical advice regarding forensic anthropology was so crucial, thank you.

I want to express my gratitude to Brian Calder for his input and his genius for marketing and thanks to Christine Horner also for her skills in copyediting and cover design.

I appreciate Anita Liston who provided historical perspective and reprint approval for photographs of John Miller and much gratitude to the Lambson family for their assistance. Along those same lines, my thanks extend to both Doug Engebretson and Gary Tietjen for their considerable insight into the histories of the Black Hills and Rama, New Mexico.

There are always people behind the scenes who surface when you need them. One such person is Gary McCarthy, whose insight into the world of publishing and book writing was remarkable. Thank you, Gary, for your advice.

Of course, without the many years of support and mentoring by Louis Gottschalk, who is now in permanent rest, Robert

Bechtel and Avinoam Sapir, the technical aspects referred to in this book would have been absent. Thank you all for your training, support, and creativity.

Finally, I would like to express my gratitude to the associates of the Santa Fe Archdiocese, Special Collections Libraries at the University of Arizona, the University of Texas at El Paso, the New Mexico Hispanic Genealogical Society and to all the previous authors and historians who traveled before me. Thank you all.

BIBLIOGRAPHY

Adams, Ramon F. *Burs Under the Saddle: A Second Look at Books and Histories of the West.* 1st edition, University of Oklahoma Press, 1964.

---. *A Fitting Death for Billy the Kid.* [1st edition, University of Oklahoma Press, 1960.

---. *More Burs Under the Saddle: Books and Histories of the West.* University of Oklahoma Press, 1979.

Airy, Helen. *Whatever Happened to Billy the Kid?* 1st edition, Sunstone Press, 1993.

Alter, Robert Edmond. *The Trail of Billy the Kid.* Belmont Tower Books, 1975.

Anaya, A. P. and James H. Earle. *I Buried Billy.* Creative Pub. Co., 1991.

Anderson, Charles D. *Outlaws of the Old West.* Mankind Pub. Co., 1973.

Arain, Mariam et al. "Maturation of the Adolescent Brain." *Neuropsychiatric Disease and Treatment*, vol. 9, 2013, pp. 449-461, ProQuest Central, doi:http://dx.doi.org/10.2147/NDT.S39776.

Arbo, Hal. *Billy the Kid, Western Outlaw.* Whitman Pub. Co., 1935.

Ball, Larry D. *Marshall John E. Sherman, Jr., 1876-1882, the United States Marshals of New Mexico and Arizona Territories, 1846-1912.* University of New Mexico Press, 1982.

Ballow, Willard. *Billy the Kid: A Graphic History.* 1st edition, Owlhoot Trail Pub. Co., 1998.

Barker, Allen. *The Billy the Kid Quiz #2.* 1st edition, A. Barker, 1996.

---. *The Kid with Fast Hands: A Carefully Researched History of Billy the Kid with Fictional Dialogue and Incidental Action.* 1st edition, A. Barker, 1993.

Black, A.P. (Ott). *The End of the Long Horn Trail.* The Selfridge Journal, 1936.

Blake, Kim D. et al. "Adolescent and Adult Issues in Charge Syndrome." *Clinical Pediatrics*, vol. 44, no. 2, 2005, pp. 151-159, ProQuest Central, https://search.proquest.com/docview/200047032?accountid=36783.

Blakemore, Sarah-Jayne. "Imaging Brain Development: The Adolescent Brain." *Neuroimage*, vol. 61, no. 2, 2012, pp. 397-406, ProQuest Central, doi:http://dx.doi.org/10.1016/j.neuroimage.2011.11.080.

Blazer, family et al. "Papers of the Blazer Family, 1857-1966 (Bulk 1870-1955)." p. 1.6 ft.

Blessing, Lee. *The Authentic Life of Billy the Kid: A Play in Two Acts.* S. French, 1980.

Bonney, William H. "Handwritten Letter to Lew Wallace." edited by Lew Wallace, Making arrangements with Wallace for the meeting. Lew Wallace collection, Indiana Historical Society, 3/20/1879 1879.

---. "Handwritten Letter to Lew Wallace." edited by Lew Wallace, Explanation of his involvement in the Death of Jim Carlyle and other troubles. Lew Wallace collection, Indiana Historical Society, 1880.

---. "Handwritten Letter to Lew Wallace." edited by Lew Wallace, Asking Wallace to keep the promise of pardon for BTK. Lew Wallace collection, Indiana Historical Society, 3/4/1881 1881.

---. "Handwritten Note to Lew Wallace." edited by Lew Wallace, Asking to see Wallace. Lew Wallace collection, Indiana Historical Society, 1/1/1881 1881.

---. "Handwritten Note to Lew Wallace." edited by Lew Wallace, Asked Wallace to keep his promise. Lew Wallace collection, Indiana Historical Society, 3/27/1881 1881.

---. "Letter Fragment." edited by Unknown, Description of criminal activities in Lincoln County. Lew Wallace collection, Indiana Historical Society, unknown/1879 1879.

---. "Letter to Friend Wilson." edited by Squire Wilson, Making arrangements for the meeting. Lew Wallace collection, Indiana Historical Society, 3/20/1879 1879.

Boomhower, Ray E. *The Sword and the Pen.* Indiana Historical Society, 2005.

Boylan, John. *The Old Lincoln County Courthouse, Lincoln, New Mexico.* Hall-Poorbaugh Press, 1960.

Breihan, Carl W. *Badmen of the Frontier Days.* McBride, 1957.

Breihan, Carl W. and Marion Ballert. *Billy the Kid; a Date with Destiny.* Hangman Press, 1970.

Brent, William. *The Complete and Factual Life of Billy the Kid.* F. Fell, 1964.

Brooks, Bill. *The Stone Garden: The Epic Life of Billy the Kid.* G.K. Hall & Co., 2001.

Burns, Walter Noble. *Billy the Kid.* Geoffrey Bles, 1930.

---. "Papers of Walter Noble Burns, 1908-1932 (Bulk 1922-1932)." p. 3.3 ft.

---. *The Saga of Billy the Kid.* Doubleday, Page & Company, 1926.

Bye, John O. *Back Trailing in the Heart of Short Grass Country.* Alexander Printing Company, 1956.

Caldwell, C. R. *Dead Right: The Lincoln County War.* Lulu.com, 2010.

Cerniglia, Luca et al. "Parental Loss During Childhood and Outcomes on Adolescents' Psychological Profiles: A Longitudinal Study: Research and Reviews Research and Reviews." *Current Psychology*, vol. 33, no. 4, 2014, pp. 545-556, ProQuest Central, doi:http://dx.doi.org/10.1007/s12144-014-9228-3.

Chamberlain, Kathleen. *In the Shadow of Billy the Kid: Susan Mcsween and the Lincoln County War.* University of New Mexico Press, 2013.

Chamberlain, Kathleen and University of New Mexico. Center for the American West. *Billy the Kid and the Lincoln County War: A Bibliography.* Center for the American West, Dept. of History, University of New Mexico, 1997.

---. *Wild Westerners: A Bibliography.* Center for the American West, Dept. of History, University of New Mexico, 1998.

Cline, Donald. *Alias Billy the Kid: The Man Behind the Legend.* 1st edition, Sunstone Press, 1986.

---. *Antrim & Billy.* Creative Pub. Co., 1990.

Coe, George W. and Nannie Hillary Harrison. *Frontier Fighter, the Autobiography of George W. Coe, Who Fought and Rode with Billy the Kid.* Houghton Mifflin Company, 1934.

Cogulu, D. et al. "Orofacial Findings and Dental Management of Williams Syndrome." *Genetic Counseling*, vol. 26, no. 4, 2015, pp. 437-442, Psychology Database, https://search.proquest.com/docview/1764121194?accountid=36783.

Commission, Old Lincoln County Memorial. *The Last Escape of Billy the Kid: A Folk Pageant Based on the History and Legend of the Lincoln County War, And.* 1965.

Corle, Edwin. *Billy the Kid.* [1st edition, Duell, 1953.

Curtis, Alexa C. "Defining Adolescence." *Journal of Adolescent and Family Health*, vol. 7, no. 2, 2015, pp. 0_1,1-39, Psychology Database, https://search.proquest.com/docview/1831353001?accountid=36783.

de Vries, Sanne L. et al. "Adolescent-Parent Attachment and Externalizing Behavior: The Mediating Role of Individual and Social Factors." *Journal of Abnormal Child Psychology*, vol. 44, no. 2, 2016, pp. 283-294, Psychology Database, doi:http://dx.doi.org/10.1007/s10802-015-9999-5.

Dresden, Donald. *The Marquis De Mores.* University of Oklahoma Press, 1970.

Duncklee, John and Penny Duncklee. *What Really Happened to Billy-the-Kid.* Barbed Wire Pub., 2002.

Dykes, Jeff. *Billy the Kid, the Bibliography of a Legend.* University of New Mexico Press, 1952.

Ealy, Taylor F. "Papers of Taylor F. Ealy, 1854-1937 (Bulk 1874-1929)." p. .4 ft.

Earle, James H. *The Capture of Billy the Kid.* Creative Pub. Co., 1988.

Edd, Karl. *Billy the Kid.* 1975.

Edwards, Daniel A. *Billy the Kid: An Autobiography.* Creative Texts Publishers, LLC, 2018.

Edwards, Harold L. *Goodbye to Billy the Kid.* Creative publishing Co., 1995.

Ellis, Wendy E. et al. "The Role of Peer Group Aggression in Predicting Adolescent Dating Violence and Relationship Quality." *Journal of Youth and Adolescence*, vol. 42, no. 4, 2013, pp. 487-499, Psychology Database, doi:http://dx.doi.org/10.1007/s10964-012-9797-0.

Engebretson, Doug. *Empty Saddles, Forgotten Names: Outlaws of the Black Hills and Wyoming.* North Plains Press, 1982.

---. *The George Axelby Gang and the Stoneville Battle.* Self, Unknown.

Etulain, Richard W. and Glenda Riley. *With Badges and Bullets: Lawmen and Outlaws in the Old West.* Fulcrum Press, 1999.

Everitt, David. *The Story of Pat Garrett and Billy the Kid.* 1st edition, Knightsbridge Pub. Co., 1990.

Fable, Edmund. *The True Life of Billy the Kid.* Creative Pub. Co., 1980.

Fackler, Elizabeth. *Billy the Kid: The Legend of El Chivato.* Forge, 1995.

Flores, Daniel. *Billy the Kid and Pat Garrett: Their Puerto De Luna Story.* CreateSpace Independent Publishing Platform, 2015.

Forrest, Earle Robert. *Papers of Earle Robert Forrest, 1895-1960, 1929-1969.*

Fulginitti, Laura C. "Exhumation, Pioneer Home Cemetery, Prescott, Az." Office of the Maricopa County Medical Examiner, June 2, 2005, p. 2.

Fuller, Mark S. *Never a Dull Moment: The Life of John Liggett Meigs.* Sunstone Press, 2015.

Fulton, Maurice G. and Geo Wilkins Kendall. "Papers of Maurice G. Fulton, 1829-1955 (Bulk 1870-1954)." p. 14 ft.

Fulton, Maurice G. and Robert N. Mullin. *History of the Lincoln County War.* University of Arizona Press, 1997.

---. *Maurice Garland Fulton's History of the Lincoln County War.* University of Arizona Press, 1968.

Galván, Adriana. "Insights About Adolescent Behavior, Plasticity, and Policy from Neuroscience Research." *Neuron*, vol. 83, no. 2, 2014, pp. 262-265, ProQuest Central, doi:http://dx.doi.org/10.1016/j.neuron.2014.06.027.

Garcia, Elbert A. *Billy the Kid's Kid, 1875-1964: The Hispanic Connection.* Los Products Press, 1999.

Gardner, Mark Lee. *To Hell on a Fast Horse: Billy the Kid, Pat Garrett and the Epic Chase to Justice in the Old West.* William Morrow, 2010.

Garrett, Pat F. *The Authentic Life of Billy, the Kid, the Noted Desperado of the Southwest, Whose Deeds of Daring and Blood Made His Name a Terror in New Mexico, Arizona and Northern Mexico.* New Mexican printing and publishing co., 1882.

Garrett, Pat F. and Maurice G. Fulton. *Authentic Life of Billy the Kid.* Macmillan, 1927.

---. *Pat F. Garrett's Authentic Life of Billy the Kid.* The Macmillan Company, 1927.

Garrett, Pat F. and Jarvis P. Garrett. *The Authentic Life of Billy the Kid.* Horn & Wallace, 1964.

Garrett, Pat F. and Frederick W. Nolan. *Pat F. Garrett's Authentic Life of Billy, the Kid.* Annotated edition, University of Oklahoma Press, 2000.

Gomber, Drew. *Lincoln County War: Heroes and Villains.* Bandillo Pub. Co., 1998.

Gottschalk, Louis A. *Content Analysis of Verbal Behavior: New Findings and Clinical Applications.* Lawrence Erlbaum Associates, Inc., 1995.

---. "Manual of Instructions for Using the Gottschalk-Gleser Content Analysis Scales." University of California Press, 1969, p. 176.

Gottschalk, Louis A. and Robert J. Bechtel. "Computerized Content Analysis of Writings of Mahatma Gandhi." *The Journal of Nervous and Mental Disease* vol. 193, no. 3, 2005.

---. "Pcad 3: Psychiatric Content Analysis and Diagnosis." 2016.

Gottschalk, Louis A. et al. "Computerized Content Analysis of Some Adolescent Writings of Napoleon Bonaparte: A Test of the Validity of the Method." *The Journal of Nervous and Mental Disease*, vol. 190, no. 8, 2002.

Gottschalk, Louis A. and Goldine C. Gleser. *The Measurement of Psychological States through the Content Analysis of Verbal Behavior.* University of California Press, 1969.

Gottschalk, L.A. and F. Lolas. "The Gottschalk-Gleser Content Analysis Method of Measuring the Magnitude of Psychological

Dimensions: Its Application in Transcultural Research." *Transcultural Psychiatric Research Review*, vol. 26, no. 2, 1989, pp. 83-777.

Gottschalk, Louis A. et al. "The Application of Computerized Content Analysis of Speech to the Diagnostic Process in a Psychiatric Outpatient Clinic." *Journal of Clinical Psychology*, vol. 53, no. 5, 1997, pp. 427-441.

Hamlin, William Lee. *The True Story of Billy the Kid; a Tale of the Lincoln County War.* Caxton Printers, 1959.

Haws, R.L. *Brushy Bill ... Just Another Billy the Kid Tall Tale?* Roy Haws Bargain Books, 2014.

Hendron, J. W. *The Story of Billy the Kid: New Mexico's Number One Desperado.* Rydal Press, 1948.

Henry, Will. *The Ballad of Billy Bonney: Being a Free Verse Folklore of the Wild Life & Dangerous Times of Billy the Kid.* 1st private press edition, Flying Coffin Press, 1984.

Hertzog, Peter. *Little Known Facts About Billy, the Kid.* Press of the Territorian, 1963.

Hudson, Bell and Mary Hudson Brothers. *Billy the Kid: The Most Hated, the Most Loved Outlaw New Mexico Ever Produced.* Hustler Press, 1949.

Hunt, Frazier. *The Tragic Days of Billy the Kid.* Hastings House, 1956.

Hyatt, H. Norman. *A Hard-Won Life.* Farcountry Press, 2014.

Hyde, Albert E. *Billy, the Kid and the Old Regime in the Southwest: An Eye-Witness Account with the Capture & Defiance of a Mob by That Notorious Desperado Dave Rudabaugh.* Frontier Book Co., 1960.

Jacobsen, Joel. *Such Men as Billy the Kid: The Lincoln County War Reconsidered.* University of Nebraska Press, 1994.

Jameson, W. C. *Billy the Kid: Investigating History's Mysteries.* Twodot Publishing, 2018.

---. *Billy the Kid: The Lost Interviews.* 2 edition, Creative Texts Publishers, 2017.

Jameson, W. C. and Frederic Bean. *The Return of the Outlaw, Billy the Kid.* Republic of Texas Press, 1998.

Jenardo, Don. *The True Story of Billy the Kid.* Saddlebag Press, 1945.

Jensen, Frances E. and Amy E. Nutt. *The Teenage Brain: A Neuroscientist's Survival Guide to Raising Adolescents and Young Adults.* HarperCollins Publishers, 2015.

Kadlec, Robert F. *They "Knew" Billy the Kid: Interviews with Old-Time New Mexicans.* 1st edition, Ancient City Press, 1987.

Keleher, William A. *Violence in Lincoln County 1869-1881.* Sunstone Press, 2007.

Klasner, Lily et al. *My Girlhood among Outlaws.* University of Arizona Press, 1972.

Koop, W. E. *Billy the Kid: The Trail of a Kansas Legend.* Kansas City Posse of the Westerners], 1965.

Lavash, Donald R. *Wilson & the Kid.* Creative Pub. Co., 1990.

Lewis, Preston. *The Demise of Billy the Kid.* Uncorrected page proofs Bantam edition, Bantam Books, 1994.

Little, Michael E. *Twelve Quiet Men.* 3rd edition, Inkwater Press, 2011.

McClintock, John S. *Pioneer Days in the Black Hills: By One of the Early Day Pioneers.* Edited by Edward L. Senn, University of Oklahoma Press, 1939.

McCown, Dennis. *The Goddess of War.* Sunstone Press, 2013.

McMurtry, Larry. *Anything for Billy.* Simon and Schuster, 1988.

Meadows, John P. *Pat Garrett and Billy the Kid as I Knew Them: Reminiscences of John P. Meadows.* Edited by John P. Wilson, 1st edition, University of New Mexico Press, 2004. John P. Wilson.

Metz, Leon C. *The Encyclopedia of Lawmen, Outlaws and Gunfighters.* Facts On File, Inc, 2003.

---. *Pat Garrett: A Story of a Western Lawman (Reprint, Revised Ed.).* University of Oklahoma Press, 1983, [1974].

Miller, Jay. *Billy the Kid Rides Again: Digging for the Truth.* Sunstone Press, 2005.

Morrison, W. M. *Billy the Kid: Las Vegas Newspaper Accounts of His Career, 1880-1881.* 1st edition, W. M. Morrison Books, 1958.

Mullin, Robert N. *The Boyhood of Billy the Kid.* Texas Western Press], 1967.

Nannemann, Allison C. et al. "Positive Behavior Supports for a Young Adult with Charge Syndrome." *Journal of Visual Impairment & Blindness (Online)*, vol. 111, no. 2, 2017, p. 175, ProQuest Central, https://search.proquest.com/docview/1876146087?accountid=36783.

Nichol, B. P. *The True Eventual Story of Billy the Kid.* Weed/Flower Press, 1970.

Nolan, Frederick W. *The Lincoln County War: A Documentary History.* Sunstone Press, 1992.

---. *The West of Billy the Kid.* University of Oklahoma Press, 1998.

Noorikhajavi, Morteza et al. "The Effect of "Parental Loss" under 18 on Developing "Mdd" in Adult Age." *International Journal of Psychiatry in Medicine*, vol. 37, no. 3, 2007, pp. 347-355, ProQuest Central, https://search.proquest.com/docview/196305276?accountid=36783.

Noppe, Illene Cupit and Lloyd D. Noppe. "Adolescent Experiences with Death: Letting Go of Immortality." *Journal of Mental Health Counseling*, vol. 26, no. 2, 2004, pp. 146-167, ProQuest Central, https://search.proquest.com/docview/198783946?accountid=36783.

Nye, Nelson C. *A Bullet for Billy the Kid.* Jove Books, 1988.

---. *Pistols for Hire; a Tale of the Lincoln County War and the West' S Most Desperate Outlaw, William (Billy, the Kid) Bonney.* The Macmillan company, 1941.

O'Connor, Richard. *Pat Garrett: A Biography of the Famous Marshal and the Killer of Billy the Kid.* [1st edition, Doubleday, 1960.

Ortuño-Sierra, Javier et al. "Different Patterns of Behavioural and Emotional Difficulties through Adolescence: The Influence of Prosocial Skills." *Anales de Psicología*, vol. 33, no. 1, 2017, pp. 48-56, Psychology Database, doi:http://dx.doi.org/10.6018/analesps.32.3.225031.

Otero, Miguel Antonio. *The Real Billy the Kid: With New Light on the Lincoln County War.* Arte Público Press, 1998.

Palmer, Michelle et al. "Understanding and Supporting Grieving Adolescents and Young Adults." *Pediatric Nursing*, vol. 42, no.

6, 2016, pp. 275-281, a2h, http://library.capella.edu/login?url=http://search.ebscohost.com/login.aspx?direct=true&db=a2h&AN=120221562&site=ehost-live&group=alumni.

Poe, John William. *The Death of Billy the Kid.* Houghton Mifflin Company, 1933.

Poe, John William and E. A. Brininstool. *The True Story of the Killing of Billy the Kid, Notorious New Mexico Outlaw.* E.A. Brininstool, 1919.

Price, G. G. *Death Comes to Billy the Kid.* Signal Pub. Co., 1940.

Priestley, Lee and Marquita Peterson. *Billy the Kid: The Good Side of a Bad Man.* Yucca Tree Press, 1993.

---. *Billy, the Kid: The Good Side of a Bad Man.* 1st edition, Arroyo Press, 1989.

Rakocy, Bill. *The Kid, Billy the Kid: The Artists and Writers Saga.* Bravo Press, 1985.

Raphael, Beverley et al. "The Impact of Parental Loss on Adolescents' Psychosocial Characteristics." *Adolescence*, vol. 25, no. 99, 1990, p. 689, ProQuest Central, https://search.proquest.com/docview/195925764?accountid=36783.

Rasch, Philip J. *Gunsmoke in Lincoln County.* Western Publications, 1997.

---. *Trailing Billy the Kid.* 1st edition, Western Publications, 1995.

---. *Warriors of Lincoln County.* Western Publications, 1998.

Riby, Deborah M. et al. "Attention to Faces in Williams Syndrome." *Journal of Autism and Developmental Disorders*, vol. 41, no. 9, 2011, pp. 1228-1239, Psychology Database, doi:http://dx.doi.org/10.1007/s10803-010-1141-5.

Rickards, Colin W. *The Gunfight at Blazer's Mill. Southwestern Studies Monograph.* Western Press, 1974.

Roberts, Calvin A. and Susan A. Roberts. *A History of New Mexico.* University of New Mexico Press, 2004.

Roegdke, Soren and Kay Busse. *Quien Es? : The True Story of Billy the Kid.* 1st edition, W.K.B. Enterprises, 1990.

Rossen, Jane Marie Teel. *Billy the Kid: The Untold Story.* Teel Rossen Pub., 1985.

Sampson, Ovetta and Gazette The. "Brain Storm/ Can't Figure out Why Teens Act The Way They Do? Some Scientists Suggest It May Be All in Their Heads." *The Gazette*, 03/11/
2002 Mar 11, 2002, p. LIFE1. ProQuest Central, https://search.proquest.com/docview/268216258?accountid=36783https://search.proquest.com/docview/268216258?accountid=36783.

Sandhu, Damanjit et al. "Adolescent Risk-Taking and Parental Attachment." *Indian Journal of Health and Wellbeing*, vol. 8, no. 11, 2017, pp. 1386-1392, ProQuest Central, https://search.proquest.com/docview/1986588826?accountid=36783.

Scanland, John Milton. *Life of Pat F. Garrett: And the Taming of the Border Outlaw: A History of the Gun Men and Outlaws, and a Life-Story of the Greatest Sheriff of the Old Southwest*. 1971.

---. *Life of Pat F. Garrett and the Taming of the Border Outlaw*. J. J. Lipsey, 1952.

Seeger, Pete et al. "The Badmen." Sound recording, Legacy, 1963.

Shumard, George. *Billy the Kid: The Robin Hood of Lincoln County?* First edition, Cambray Enterprises, 1969.

Simmons, Marc. *Stalking Billy the Kid*. Sunstone Press, 2006.

Siringo, Charles A. *History of "Billy the Kid."* 1920.

---. *History of "Billy the Kid."* Steck-Vaughn Co., 1967.

Siringo, Charles A. and the University of New Mexico. Center for the American West. *History of "Billy the Kid."* University of New Mexico Press, 2000.

Smith, Ashley R. et al. "Peers Influence Adolescent Reward Processing, but Not Response Inhibition." *Cognitive, Affective and Behavioral Neuroscience*, vol. 18, no. 2, 2018, pp. 284-295, ProQuest Central, doi:http://dx.doi.org/10.3758/s13415-018-0569-5.

Sonnichsen, C. L. and William Vincent Morrison. *Alias Billy the Kid "... I Want to Die a Free Man ...".* University of New Mexico Press, 1955.

Spicer, Jack. *Billy the Kid*. Oyster Press, 1975.

---. *Billy the Kid*. Enkidu Surrogate, 1959.

Sussillo, Mary V. "Beyond the Grave-Adolescent Parental Loss: Letting Go and Holding On." *Psychoanalytic Dialogues*, vol. 15, no. 4, 2005, pp. 499-527, ProQuest Central, https://search.proquest.com/docview/233320484?accountid=3678 3.

Swartley, Ron. *The Billy the Kid Travel Guide: In the Footsteps of America's Most Famous Outlaw.* Frontier Image Press, 1999.

Tanikawa, Shuntar and Harold Wright. *Billy the Kid.* Bieler Press, 1980.

Tatum, Stephen. *Inventing Billy the Kid: Visions of the Outlaw in America, 1881-1981.* 1st edition, University of New Mexico Press, 1982.

---. *Inventing Billy the Kid: Visions of the Outlaw in America, 1881-1981.* 1st University of Arizona Press paperbound edition, University of Arizona Press, 1997.

Tunnell, Dale L. "Forensic Psycholinguistic Methodology Basic Course." Training Manual, 2006.

---. "Report of Investigation: John Miller." translated by Professional Standards Bureau, Arizona Department of corrections, 2003.

---. *Voice Frequency Analysis of Cognitive Stress Differences between Men and Women During an Episodic Deception Task.* Proquest LLC, 2012.

Tunstill, William A. *Billy the Kid and Me Were the Same.* Western History Research Center, 1988.

Turner, George E. *Secrets of "Billy the Kid."* Baxter Lane Co., 1974.

Tuska, Jon. *Billy the Kid, a Handbook.* University of Nebraska Press, 1986.

---. *Billy the Kid, His Life and Legend.* Greenwood Press, 1994.

---. *Billy the Kid: A Bio-Bibliography.* Greenwood Press, 1983.

Tyrka, Audrey R. et al. "Childhood Parental Loss and Adult Psychopathology: Effects of Loss Characteristics and Contextual Factors." *International Journal of Psychiatry in Medicine*, vol. 38, no. 3, 2008, pp. 329-344, ProQuest Central, https://search.proquest.com/docview/196305987?accountid=3678 3.

Utley, Robert Marshall. *Billy the Kid: A Short and Violent Life.* University of Nebraska Press, 1989.

---. *Four Fighters of Lincoln County*. 1st edition, University of New Mexico Press, 1986.

---. *High None in Lincoln: Violence on the Western Frontier*. University of New Mexico Press, 1987.

Valdez, Jannay P. and Bobby E. Hefner. *Billy the Kid: "Killed" in New Mexico--Died in Texas*. Outlaw Publications, 1995.

Vargas, Robert. "Being in "Bad" Company: Power Dependence and Status in Adolescent Susceptibility to Peer Influence." *Social Psychology Quarterly*, vol. 74, no. 3, 2011, pp. 310-332, Psychology Database, https://search.proquest.com/docview/908976351?accountid=36783.

Walker, Dale L. *Legends and Lies: Great Mysteries of the American West*. 1st edition, Forge, 1997.

Walker, J. P. *The American Old West: Gangs, Outlaws and Gunfights*. 1st edition, Lulu Press, 2015.

Wallis, Michael. *Billy the Kid: The Endless Ride*. W. W. Norton and Company, 2007.

Walz, Edgar A. *"Retrospection."* s.n., 1931.

Weddle, Jerry. *Antrim Is My Stepfather's Name: The Boyhood of Billy the Kid*. Arizona Historical Society, 1993.

Whitlow, Duane. *Lincoln County Diary*. 1st edition, Sunstone Press, 1992.

Wilson, John P. *Pat Garrett and Billy the Kid as I Knew Them: Reminiscences of John P. Meadows*. University of New Mexico Press, 2004.

Wilson, R. Michael. *Great Stagecoach Robberies of the Old West*. Morris Book Publishing, LLC, 2007.

Wurlitzer, Rudolph. *Pat Garrett and Billy the Kid*. New American Library, 1973.

INDEX

A

abandonment, 62, 63, 64, 70, 71
abilities: cognitive, xi, 71
abnormalities, 77
abuse, 66, 189, 199
acetabulum, 157
achievement, 191, 192
Achievement Strivings, 181, 183, 184, 186, 187, 188, 192
activity: gang-like, 6
adjudications, 55
Administrative Investigations Unit, 113
administrative records, 58
admiration, 63
adolescence, 54, 61, 71, 77, 84
adolescent, xi, 54, 60, 67, 68, 70, 84
adolescent brain, xi, 54, 68
adulthood, xi, 61, 62, 69, 72
adverse criticism, 189
advertising, 85
aging brain, 69
Airy, Helen, 116, 122, 124, 126, 127, 131, 135, 136, 139, 147, 149, 154, 158, 171
Albuquerque, NM, 132
Alderbeau, M. C., 163
alternate universe, 57
altruistic, 64
Ambivalent Hostility, 181, 182, 184, 185, 186, 188, 190
amnesty, 31

analgesics, 199
anatomical abnormalities, 60
anatomy, xi, 68, 77, 152
anecdotal accounting, 59
Angel, Frank Warner, 27
anger, 71
antagonism, 116, 190
antemortem, 157
anthropometric, 79
antidepressants, 199
Anton Chico, 31, 37, 148, 160, 168
Antrim: Catherine, 4, 5, 117; Henry, 4, 5, 6, 9, 25, 61; Joseph (Josie), 5
anxiety, 71, 189, 196, 199
Apaches, 14
apprehension, 25
Arizona, 111, 114
Arizona Department of Corrections, 111, 112
Arizona Republic, 120
arousal, 70, 189
Artesia, NM, 56
Ashcroft, Rulon, 136
asocial impulses, 190
assaultive, 190
assessment, xi, 170
assessments: medical, xi, 68, 77, 118, 124, 137, 157, 172; psychological, xi
Asymmetric features, 152
asymmetrical, 79
Atkins, George, 9
attention-deficit-hyperactive, 199
attestations, 6
authority, 12, 20, 21, 36, 69, 127

autonomic nervous system, 189
autopsies, 77
Avants, Bundy, 52
avarice, 18
avoidance, 190
Axelbee, George. See Exelbee, George
Axtell, Governor, 12, 17, 19, 21, 28
Axtell, Samuel B., 21

B

backup, vii, 53, 54
Baker, Frank, 14, 19, 21, 87
barefooted, 44
bareheaded, 44
Barela, Mariano, 11, 15
battle, 12, 24, 27, 29, 30, 37, 132
Battle of Fritz Ranch, 26
Battle of Lincoln, 18, 29
Baxter, Carl, 132, 133, 147
behavior, 61, 64, 69, 70, 71, 73, 124, 187, 188, 195, 198
Bell, J. W., 39
Bell, James, 111
Bertillon, Alphonse, 79
bilingual, 55
Black River, 27
Blazer's Mill, 24, 132
bloodshed, 30
Bonaparte, Napoleon, 85, 208
Bond, Atheling, 125, 136, 158
Bonita, AZ, 8, 88
Bonney: William H., vi, ix, 4, 7, 10, 16, 19, 21, 31, 32, 35, 45, 65, 68, 86, 88, 89, 90, 93, 94, 95, 125, 139, 140, 142, 174, 175, 204, 209, 211
Bowdre, Charlie, 10, 16, 21, 24, 25, 30, 34, 38, 39, 64, 146
Box Elder Creek, MT, 160
Boys, 9, 10, 12, 16, 19

Brady, William, 12, 19, 21, 33, 39, 64, 65
brain development: adolescent, xi
Brazil, Manuel, 43
breast cancer, 199
Brewer, David A., 56
Brewer, Dick, 10, 14, 16, 17, 21, 24, 63
bridge: Brooklyn, 3
Bristol, Judge Warren, 21, 39, 65
British Recruiting Mission, 139
broad-brimmed hat. See Sombrero
Brown, "Bad Land Charlie", 162
Brown, "Bronco" Charlie, 164
bruxism, 199
Buckeye, AZ, 113, 132, 134, 154
burial, 27, 44, 113, 117, 119, 125, 162
Burns, Walter Noble, 144, 205
business, 7, 19, 25, 33, 85, 88, 160
Bustamante, Feliz, 138
butcher knife, 44, 54

C

Cacouse, Jesus, 141, 144, 170
Cahill, 8, 9
Cahill, Frank "Windy", 9
Cain, Paul, 58
camaraderie, 72
Campbell, Hank, 162
Campbell, Jack, 164
Campbell, William, 32
Capitan Mountains, vii
Carlyle, Jim, 36, 37, 204
carpenter shop, 57
Case, Robert, 16
Case, Will, 16, 95, 209
Casey, Ellen, 15, 16
Casey, Lily, 16
castration, 189
casualty, 63

Catron, Thomas B., 21, 28
Cattle King, 12
Caypless, Edgar, 65
Cemetery: Pioneer Home, v, 113, 116, 154, 207
cerebral glucose metabolic rates, 199
Chain Gain, 9
Chapman, Huston, 32
Chávez y Chávez, 30
child development, 69
chimney, 8
Chinese, 8
Chisum ranch, 29, 30
Chisum, Jim, 34, 35
Chisum, John, 12, 16, 25, 34, 35, 66, 87
cholecystectomy, 199
Christmas Eve, 38
church: Presbyterian, 5
clavicles, 157
Clayton Wells, NM, 164, 168
clemency, 64, 145
cliff notes, 45
clinic theory, 197
Coe, Frank, 14, 26, 27
Coe, George, 14, 25, 26
Cognitive, 75, 181, 182, 184, 185, 186, 188, 191, 213, 214
coherence, 190
collateral, 15
collections: historical, 3
collectively, 57
Colorado: Denver, 6
companionship, 62, 63
comprehensive, 45
compulsions, 189
concha, 79, 152
conclusions, xi, 58, 81, 115
condemnation, 189
conditions: psychiatric, xi, 85

conspiracy, ix, 19, 50, 125
conspiracy theories, 50
constitutionality, 19
contracts, 12, 19, 25, 129
contributors: pathological, xi, 157; physiological, xi; psychological, xi, 68, 85, 123, 195, 196, 197, 198, 231
conviction, v, 25, 65
Copeland, John, 25
Corbet, Sam, 24
coroner's jury, 9, 57
corpses, 77
corroboration, 4, 17
corrupt legal system, 24
Cortisol. *See* neurochemical
courthouse, 3, 39, 41, 123, 162
Covert Hostility, 188
cranial, 78, 83
Crawford, Charlie, 16
Creasy, Frank, 142, 151, 168
Creasy, Frank Burrard "Bert", 139
criminal investigations, 85
critical thinking, x, 149
crusader, 60, 64, 84
Cunningham, William, 164
Custer County, MT, 163

D

Darwin's tubercle, 81
data: birth, 4; critical, 3; demographic, 3, 147
daughter, 11, 15, 16, 58, 148
Dave Rudabaugh, 33, 36, 209
Davis, George, 25, 37, 87
dead right there, 41
Deadwood, SD, 161, 162, 163
Death, 4, 8, 18, 34, 45, 46, 47, 48, 106, 133, 147, 150, 151, 159, 181, 182,

183, 184, 185, 186, 187, 188, 192, 203, 204, 211, 212
death scene, 44
death warrant, 64
debate, vi, xi, 53, 174
deception, 57, 115
decision center. See frontal lobes
decision-making, xi, 70
declaration, 12, 19
deconstruction, 55
delinquent, 8, 61
dental overcrowding, 82
Denver, 6
Department of Interior, 25
Department of Justice, 25, 27
Dependency, Strivings, 188
depression, 190, 192, 196, 199
Depression, 181, 182, 183, 184, 185, 187, 188, 191, 192, 194
deterrent factors, 61
diabetes mellitus, 199
Dias, Solomon, 138
Diffuse anxiety, 189
Diffuse Anxiety, 181, 182, 183, 185, 186, 188
Director, 113, 118, 119, 231
directories: local, 7
Dirty Dave. See Dave Rudabaugh
disappointment, 64, 66
discrepancies, 51, 56, 57, 124, 142, 174
disorders, 82, 199; congenital, xi
distortion, 195
distress, 71
DNA, 117, 118, 119, 155, 156, 157
documentation, x, 4, 7, 16, 122, 142, 143
Dolan, James, 19
Dolan, Jimmy, 12
dopamine, 70
Dr. Ealy, 24

droopier, 79
DRT. *See* Dead Right There
Dudley, Col., 27, 29, 30, 33
Duffy, John, 163
dying declaration, 9
Dyke, Jeanine, 118, 119

E

Eagle Creek, 16
earlobe, 81
ears, 79, 152
Edwards, Buck, 36
El Morro, NM, 125, 128
El Paso, TX, 132, 165
Ellis corrals, 26
Ellis house, 26
elongation, 79
Elvis, 68
embarrassment, 189
embellishment, x, 114, 123
embezzlement, 25
emotion, 71
emotions, 69, 70, 199
English, 39, 54, 55, 58, 61, 65, 136, 157
entitlement, 193
environment, 45, 54, 60, 84, 162; structured, 5; unstructured, 6, 195
environmental stimuli, 69
equalizers, 61
Eriacho, Jesus, 128, 129
escapades, 8, 73, 164
Escape, 39, 91, 206
escaped, 8, 37, 66, 86, 140
euphoria, 66
evaluation, xi, 45, 71, 194
Evans, Jesse, 9, 10, 12, 14, 15, 16, 19, 25, 32, 87, 88

evidence, xi, 5, 6, 7, 18, 59, 61, 76, 82, 116, 122, 123, 124, 147, 149, 157, 172
evolution, xi, 84
excavation, 118, 119, 154, 155, 156, 157
Exelbee Gang, 162
Exelbee, Francis, 160
Exelbee, George, 160, 162, 163, 164, 165, 168, 170, 171
Exelbee, William, vi, ix, 4, 5, 6, 7, 12, 19, 21, 25, 32, 33, 39, 45, 64, 65, 68, 86, 90, 93, 119, 125, 139, 140, 142, 143, 157, 160, 161, 170, 204, 205, 208, 209, 210, 211, 212, 213, 214
exemption, 33
exonerated, 25, 33
eyelids, 79, 82, 152
eyewitness, 31

F

facial features, 76, 77, 170
facial muscles, 79
fair trial, 33
falsifiability, 115
family: Tunstall, 10, 15, 16, 17, 18, 19, 20, 21, 22, 24, 25, 27, 31, 33, 63
fatal, 53
Father Barrera, 126
Father Herrera, 127
fear, 71, 147, 190
Federal Law Enforcement Training Center, 56
Feliz ranch, 16
Feliz River, 15
fibrocartilage, 79
Fiddler, Ben, 161
Finan, Jack, 34

findings: evidentiary, x
firearms, 61, 71, 72
flexibility, 69
floorplan, 51
folktale, x
forensic anthropology, 68
Fort Grant, AZ, 8, 9
Fort Meade, SD, 163
Fort Stanton, 12, 23, 27, 30, 33, 39
Fort Sumner, v, 30, 33, 34, 35, 37, 38, 41, 42, 43, 50, 52, 55, 57, 58, 64, 66, 67, 71, 73, 90, 112, 122, 124, 125, 128, 130, 131, 136, 145, 146, 160
Fort Wingate, NM, 131
Fountain, Albert J., 65
frame of reference, viii, xi, 45
freebooter, 161
French, Jim, 21, 23, 24, 30, 31
frontal cortex, 70
frontal lobes, 69, 71
funerals, 54

G

Gallup Archdioceses, 127
Garrett, Elizabeth, 58, 207
Garrett, Pat, v, xi, 37, 39, 44, 50, 58, 66, 73, 114, 116, 122, 125, 126, 127, 131, 141, 143, 144, 145, 146, 158, 168, 207, 208, 210, 211, 215
Garrett, Patrick Floyd. *See* Garrett, Pat
Gatling gun, 30
Gauss, Gottfried, 17
genealogy,, 3
General Land Office, 129
Georgetown, NM, 171
Ghandi, Mahatma, 85
Gleser, Goldine, 85
Gonzales, Ignacio, 30

Goodnight-Loving Trail, 160
Goodwin, Lieutenant, 8, 27, 89
Gottschalk, Louis a., 85
Grady, Alex, 162, 164
grammatical, 197
grand jury, 25, 33
Grant, Joe, 34
grassland, 12
Greathouse Trading Post, 36
grounded, 61, 70
Group: Antrim, 5, 6, 7, 8, 9, 62, 140, 142, 143, 205, 215; McCarty, 6
Guadalajara, 58
Guadalupe Mountains, 14
guardhouse, 27
gubernatorial decree, 21
guilt, 65, 189
Guilt, 181, 182, 183, 185, 186, 188
Guiterrez, Maria Marcelena, 148
gunshot, 9, 41, 165
gunshot wound, 9, 165
Gurule, Antonia, 148
Gurule, Maria Antonia, 148
gut feeling, x
Gutierrez, Celsa, 44

H

hangman's noose, 40, 50, 165
Hardin, John Wesley, 165
Hargrove, Bob, 34
Harris, Jack, 164
Hashknife Ranch, 160
Health/Sickness, 181, 183, 184, 185, 187, 188
hearsay, 126
helix, 79, 81
Herrera, Fernando, 30
Hettinger, ND, 161
Hill, Tom, 19, 87
Hindman, George, 19, 22
historian, ix, x
historical event, x
Historical Society: Indiana, 86, 114, 145, 204, 205, 215
history: paternal, 7
Holocaust, 68
homestead, 129
Homestead Act, 129
Hondo River, 15
Hope, 181, 182, 184, 185, 186, 188, 191
hopeless, 199
Hopelessness, 181, 182, 184, 185, 186
hormone-driven emotions, 69
Horse Head Canyon, NM, 142
hostility, 188, 190, 196
Hostility Inward, 181, 182, 185, 186, 188
Hostility Outward, 188, 192
housewife, 7
howitzer, 30
Hudspeth, William, 119, 157
Human Relations, 181, 183, 184, 185, 187, 188, 192
humanity, 63
humiliation, 189
Huntsville Prison, TX, 165
Hurley, John, 36
hypochondriacal symptoms, 189
hypothesis, 115

I

ideology, 60
illustrations, ix, 68, 81
immigrants, 5
impairment: cognitive, 199
impatient, 53

impetuous, 84
impulsiveness, 69
impulsivity, 69
inadequacy, 189
inadmissible, 126
incarceration, 76
incompetence, 53
inconsistencies, 58, 111, 126, 142
incorporation, 7
independence, 60, 62, 70
independently, 58
Indiana, 4, 7, 86, 114, 204, 205
Indianapolis, IN, 7, 143
indictments, 33
infallible, 55
infirmary, 9
innate intellect, 61
innominate, 157
insurance claim, 25
Intellectual Impairment, 191
inter-coder reliability coefficient, 188
interlopers, 19
investigator, ix, 51, 56, 111, 112, 114, 115, 147, 172
irrational, 55
ischiopubic ramus, 157
ischium, 157

J

Jackson, Frank, 163
jail, 8, 14, 16, 21, 33, 39, 40, 140, 145
Jameson, W. C., 51
Jones, Barbara, 14
journals, 77
journey, vi, 6, 129, 130
judgment, 53, 54, 62, 68
jury, 19, 25, 39, 65, 172
Justice of the Peace, 19, 21, 27

K

Kansas, 6, 8, 139, 143, 210;
    Coffeyville, 4, 140, 142, 143;
    Wichita, 6, 7, 8, 143
kill zone, 41
killed like a dog, 89
Kimbrell, George, 33
Kimbrell, John, 35
Kruling, "Dutch" Charlie, 26

L

La Mesilla, NM, 11, 33, 39
lack of attention, 69
Lambson, Eugene, 131, 132, 134
Las Cruces, NM, 65, 141, 145
Las Vegas Jail, 37
Las Vegas policemen. *See* Dave Rudabaugh and Tom Pickett
Las Vegas. NM, 33, 37, 90, 124, 126, 128, 130, 147, 210
laundry, 5, 7, 8
lawlessness, vii, 19, 32
lawmen, 19, 43, 55, 57, 66
Lawrence County, SD, 163
leadership, 63
learning capacity, 71
learning disabilities, 69
legend, x, 45, 50, 52, 162, 175
Leonard, Ira, 39, 65
letters, 3, 39, 61, 64, 68, 76, 84, 86, 114, 115, 122, 123, 132
lexical cues, 196
Liberty, AZ, 134, 136
lightheartedness, 64
limitations, 61
Lincoln County Courthouse, 66, 111, 112, 205

Lincoln County War, viii, 12, 18, 34, 63, 205, 206, 207, 208, 209, 211
linguistic theory, 197
livestock, 9, 10, 12, 31, 71, 139, 168
Llano Estacado, 15, 33
lobe, 79, 81, 152
lobule, 81
logic, 54
logicality of thinking, 190
loneliness, 62, 71
Long, Jack, 22
Long, John, 25
Longworth, Thomas B., 36
loyalty, 17, 18, 63
luck, 57
lucky, 4, 54, 57, 112

M

Mabry, Thomas, 175
Mackie, John R., 8
Malpais, viii
management, 85, 118
manufactured, 55
Maricopa County Prosecutor, 120
Maricopa County Sheriff, 134
marketing, 85
marriage, 5, 127, 130, 143, 148, 171
Martinez, Atanacio, 20, 30
Martz, "Dutch" Martin, 17
masochism, 190
mastectomy, 199
Mathews, Billy, 16, 22, 23
Maurice Fulton Collection, 114
Maxwell, Deluvina, 56
Maxwell, Paulita, 43
Maxwell, Pete, 31, 35, 43, 51, 112, 124, 127, 146
Mayhan, N. M. J., 158
McCabe, Abner, 15

McCarthy, William, 161, 164, 170
McCarty: Henry, 4, 5, 6, 7, 8, 9, 21, 25, 26, 30, 61, 87, 143, 154, 209; Joseph, 5
McCarty, Catherine, 4, 5, 6, 7, 143
McCarty, William Henry, 4
McCloskey, Bill, 17
McDaniels, Jimmy, 10
McKinney, "Kip", 43
McMahan, Frank, 165
McNab, Frank, 21, 26, 27
McSween, Alexander, 10, 15, 19, 20, 23, 25, 30, 34
McSween, Susan, 30, 32, 66
medicine, 85
Memory Lane Cemetery, Silver City, NM, 171
mental health, 85, 86
mental states, xi
methodological, 68
methodology: investigative, xi, 51, 114; modern, x, xi, 84, 115, 118; scientific, x, xi, 81, 84, 112, 115, 116, 118, 152, 193
Metz, Leon, ix, 143
Mexican sombrero, 38
Middleton, John, 21, 30
midface, 82
militia, 32
Miller, Isadora, 116, 122, 124, 125, 126, 127, 129, 130, 132, 133, 134, 136, 138, 147, 148, 149, 158, 168, 171, 172
Miller, John, 68, 111, 113, 114, 115, 116, 117, 118, 119, 122, 124, 125, 126, 128, 129, 131, 132, 134, 135, 136, 139, 141, 142, 143, 144, 145, 146, 148, 149, 152, 153, 154, 156, 157, 158, 165, 168, 170, 171, 172, 174, 175, 214
Miller, Max, 127, 135, 154

miners, 5, 131
mining, 5
miracle herd, 12
misjudgments, 53, 57
mistaken identity, 38, 58
moniker, 8
monopoly, 12
moral disapproval, 189
morphology, 79, 80
Morris, Harvey, 30
Morton, Billy, 14, 19
Morton, Buck, 16, 21
motivation, 8, 53, 63, 192, 193
Mrose, Helen Beulah, 165
Mrose, Martin, 164, 165, 168
murder, 19, 25, 28, 32, 33, 39, 65
Murphy, L. G., 12
Murphy, Lawrence, 25
Mutilation, 181, 182, 183, 184, 185, 186, 187, 188, 189, 192

N

Narbeau, Max, 160
Narcissistic, 193
National Archives, 51
neural control systems: arousal, 70
neurobiology, 84
neurochemical: cortisol, 71
neuropsychiatric, 188, 199
neuropsychiatry, 198
neuropsychopharmacology, 199
neuroscientists, 67
neurotransmitters, 69
New Mexicans, 29, 210
New Mexico Hispanic Genealogical Research Center, 148
New Mexico Mounted Patrol, vii
New York, 4, 139, 162
New York City, 4

newcomers, 5
Nixon, Richard, xi
Nolan, Frederick, ix, 3, 114, 143
nuptial vows, 6
nursing, 24, 85

O

O'Folliard, Tom, 30, 31, 33, 37, 39, 64
O'Hara, Jack, 163
O'Keefe, James, 14
obfuscation, 58
Office of Governor, 113
Olinger, Robert, 37, 39, 66, 111
Ontario Provincial Police, CA, 140
Ontario Provincial Police, CAN, 139
Ontario Provincial Police, ON, CA, 139
open-ended statements, 85
optimism, 191
os coxae, 157
Osage Indian Trust Act of 1869, 6
ossified, 77
osteoarthritis, 156, 157
Overt Hostility, 188

P

Padilla, Jose Padilla, 148
Padilla, Jose Pedro, 148
Padilla, maria Antonia, 148
palsy, 79, 82
pardon, 33, 39, 141, 144, 145, 168, 175, 204
pardoned, 31, 64
parental guidance, 8
participants, x, 76, 114, 116
patent, 129
pathologists, xi, 77
pathology, 157

Patrón, Juan, 32, 33
Pecos River, viii, 16, 37, 160, 164, 165
pectoral muscles, 77
pectoral saddle, 77
peer pressure, 70
Peñasco River, 21
Peppin, George, 22, 28, 30
perception: risk, 45, 69, 71
persona, 45, 82, 85
personal disorganization. *See* schizophrenia
personalities, x, 62, 68, 76
personality, viii, xi, 17, 71, 196
perspective, 24, 45, 69
petition, 7, 28, 135
pharmacokinetics, 199
Phoenix, AZ, 113, 132, 134, 231
physicians, xi, 137
physiological, xi, 56, 69, 76, 123, 197
Pickett, Tom, 33
Pioneer Home, 113, 116, 118, 119, 154, 156, 157, 158, 207
pioneers, viii, x, 114, 122, 149, 172
planning: reasoned, x
pneumonia, 154
Poe, John, 43, 58, 127, 146
politics, v, 7
positron emission tomography, 199
posse, 19, 25, 26, 27, 29, 31, 36, 37, 43, 65, 124, 125, 126, 127, 131, 141, 144, 146, 163, 164, 168
Posse Comitatus Act, 29
postmortem, 156
prefrontal cortex, 71
pregnant, 43
premeditated murder, 65
Prescott, AZ, 113, 116, 118, 119, 134, 154, 207
presumption of innocence, 39
prisoners, 40
Probate Court, 134, 135

proclamation, 21, 28, 31
professional, 56, 57, 60
Professional Standards Bureau, 111, 214
profiles: conjecture-based, 3
property, 6, 7, 92, 128, 129, 134, 135
prospecting, 5
Protrusion, 152
protrusive, 79, 82, 152
Pruden, Jesse, 162, 163
pseudo-sleuths, 79
psyche, 52, 61
psychiatric, xi, 82, 85, 194
Psychiatric Content Analysis and Diagnosis, 187, 208
psychiatry, 85
psychoactive, 199
psychoanalysis, 85
psychoanalytic, 189, 197
psychobiological, 187, 189
psychodynamic psychotherapy, 198
psycholinguistics, 112, 231
psychology, 68, 76, 85, 112, 189, 198
Psychomotor Retardation, 181, 182, 184, 185, 186, 192
psychosocial, 72
psychotherapeutic, 198
ptosis, 82, 152
Ptosis, 82, 152
pubescent, 60
pubis, 157
Puerto de Luna, 31
Purington, George, 12, 30

Q

quasi-official capacity, 51
Quemado, NM, 130
Quien es?, 44
quitclaim, 129

R

Ramah, NM, 122, 125, 127, 128, 131, 132, 134, 139, 141, 142, 144, 147, 171
reasoning: deductive, x
rebellion, 69
recalcitrant behavior, 69
reconstruction, 55
Regulators, 21, 24, 25, 26, 27, 28, 29, 30, 31, 63
regurgitated, 68
relevance, 52, 76, 115, 138, 172
Reliability, 189
replevin, 65
researcher, x, 172, 231
researchers, x, 3
research-testing: validated, xi
reservation, 8, 12, 88, 163
Reserve, NM, 125, 128, 130
resilience, 71
resurrection, 59
revelations: intangible, xi; tangible, xi
revenge, 18, 19, 31, 34, 63, 161
reverse psychology, 41
reward, 25, 37, 54, 70, 71, 72, 73, 140, 141, 145, *See* neural control systems
ribcage, 157
risky behavior, 54, 62, 66, 70, 71
Roberts,, 175
Roberts, "Brushy Bill", 68
Roberts, Buckshot, 24
Romero, Desiderio, 31
Roswell, NM, 35, 37, 43, 160
Rudolf, Milnor, 35
Ruidoso, 24
rustling, 10, 31, 35, 43, 62
Ryan, Joe, 163

S

Sacramento mountains, viii
Saiz, Juan, 148
Saiz, Manuel Antonio, 148
Saiz, Maria Delores, 148
San Carlos, 8
San Jose Church, NM, 148
San Miguel, 31, 35, 131
San Miguel County, 31
San Patricio, 27, 29, 86, 88
Santa Fe Archdiocese, 126
Santa Fe Ring, vii, 12, 21, 33, 65
Santa Fe, NM, 5, 6, 143
Sapir, Avinoam, 231
Saunders, James A. "AB\, 26
scapulae, 157
schizophrenia: social alienation-personal disorganization, 191, 199
school, 5, 7, 192
schoolteacher, 5
Scientific Content Analysis, 231
scoliosis, 78
Scott, Winfred, 66
Scroggins, John, 25, 30
Scurlock, Doc, 10, 21, 25, 27, 30, 31
seasoned officers, 54
Sederwall, Steve, 51, 55, 111, 120
Segovia, Namual, 25
Self-Accusation, 181, 182, 184, 185, 186
sentenced, 39
separation, 4, 70, 189
Separation, 181, 182, 183, 184, 185, 186, 187, 188, 192
September, 1874, 8
septicemia, 137
Seven Rivers, 14, 15, 16, 25, 26, 27, 58, 87, 89, 165

shackled, 39
shame, 189
Shame, 181, 182, 183, 185, 186, 188
Sheriff Garrett. *See* Garrett, Pat
Sherman, John, 33, 35
shootout, 18, 124, 126, 140, 158, 164, 168
shotgun, 66
shoulder saddle, 77, 153
shoulders., 76, 77
significant markers, 69
Silver City, NM, 4, 5, 7, 8, 62, 140, 143, 171
Siringo, Charles, 144
sister-in-law, 44
six-shooter, 54, 60
skeletal structure, 77, 82
slab of meat, 44
slope, 77
Smith, John, 21
Smith, Lieutenant, 27, 88, 213
snapshot, 45, 86
sociology, 85
Somatic Concerns, 181, 182, 184, 185, 187, 192
South Spring ranch, 16
Southwest, 12, 208, 209, 213
Spanish, 15, 17, 24, 54, 58, 136, 146
Spearfish, SD, 162, 163, 164
Special Collections Branch, 114
spontaneous joy, 69
stability, 62
Staked Plains, 15
standardized, 85, 196
statements: global, x
Stephens, Steve, 25, 30
Stewart, Frank, 65
Stinking Springs, 35, 37, 64, 65, 146
Stone, Lou, 163
Stoneville, MT, 160, 163, 164, 168, 207

storyteller, x, 115
Street Arabs, 5
strength, 61
stress, 56, 69, 71
Stress, 71, 214
Sullivan, Tom, 111, 120
supper time, 40
surgeon, 9
surgery, 77, 81, 85
survival, x, 12, 31, 50, 67, 191
synapsis, 71

T

Taiban, NM, 43
Taos, NM, 58
target-rich environment, 10
technology: assessment, xi
Tecklenburg, Herman, 130, 131, 136
testimony, 33, 65, 123, 125, 138
Texas, 15, 31, 34, 35, 87, 117, 118, 165, 170, 171, 175, 209, 210, 215
Texas Red. See Joe Grant
theory: journalistic, 4
thievery, 10, 12
Tietjen, Gary, 122, 124, 146
tintype, 60, 68, 76, 77, 79, 81, 152
To fit in, 72
To measure up, 72
To stand out, 72
To take hold, 73
tomes, 3, 122
tormentors, 61
Toronto, ON, CA, 139
Total Hostility Outward, 188
tragus, 81
tranquilizers, 199
transient, 190, 191, 192, 193
trap, 37
treatment, 6, 9, 40

trial, 12, 27, 33, 39, 57, 65, 141, 144, 163
trunk, 132, 133, 134, 135
tuberculosis, 4, 6, 143, 160
Tunstall ranch, 15
Tunstall, John, 10, 14, 17, 18, 19, 25
Tuttle, Henry, 162, 164

U

U.S. Marshal, 33, 35
unbalanced, 84
United States Attorney, 29
University of Arizona, 114
unprofessional, 57
unresolved, 50
Upson, Ash, 143
Utley, Robert, ix, 114, 143

V

validity, x, 130, 188, 189, 199
vengeance, 63
veracity, 53, 149
vertebrae, 156, 157
vigilante committee, 164
Village Arabs, 8
vulnerabilities, 69
VVN ranch, 165

W

Waite, Fred, 17, 20, 21
Wallace, Lew, xi, 31, 37, 61, 64, 68, 86, 88, 90, 93, 95, 114, 115, 145, 185, 186, 187, 204

warrior, 29
washstand, 56
water, 12, 129
Webb, John Joshua, 37
Whitaker, Forest, 82
white guys, 55
White Oaks, 36, 37, 43, 90, 125
Whitehill, 8
Wild, Azariah, 35
wildfire, 19
Willard, Cap, 163
Willard, Fred, 163
Wilson, Squire, 19, 21, 32, 33, 36, 86, 204, 210, 215
Winchester, 23, 41, 60, 161, 164
Winchester rifle, 23, 60
Windenmann, John, 27
withdrawal, 189, 190
witnesses, 5, 65, 76, 133, 143, 162
womb, 77
workbench, 57, 116, 117
worry, 71, 197
Wortley Hotel, 40
writing, 19, 21, 61, 86, 124, 129

Y

Yavapai County, AZ, 118, 134, 156
Yerby ranch, 34
Yerby, Thomas, 34

Z

Zuni mountains, NM, 128

ABOUT THE AUTHOR

DR. DALE TUNNELL was born in Powell, Wyoming in 1951. He is a decorated Vietnam veteran, married and now living a retired lifestyle in Phoenix, Arizona.

Trained in psycholinguistics and psychological content analysis, Dale is a retired law enforcement officer with over forty years of service with federal, state, and local agencies. He earned his Master of Arts Degree in Management from Webster University and his Doctor of Philosophy Degree in Psychology from Capella University.

Dale received Beginning, Advanced, and Stage II training in Scientific Content Analysis (SCAN) from Avinoam Sapir at the Laboratory for Scientific Interrogation, in Phoenix, Arizona, and for a brief period, was an instructor for LSI. He also mentored under Louis Gottschalk, MD, Ph.D., at the University of California at Irvine, where he acquired his expertise in Psychiatric Content Analysis and Diagnosis.

Dale served as a Senior Researcher for Nemesysco, Ltd, Netanya, Israel, and is recognized internationally as an expert in Layered Voice Analysis. He was also the Director of Forensic Intelligence and Research with Halcyon Group International.

Dale's interest in the American West began in 1976 when he first worked as a deputy sheriff in Lincoln County, New Mexico. He is an author and active member of the American Psychological Association and the Linguistic Society of America.

www.ingramcontent.com/pod-product-compliance
Lightning Source LLC
Chambersburg PA
CBHW052019070526
44584CB00016B/1814